MORAL SOCIOLOGY
for a NEW EPOCH

MORAL SOCIOLOGY
for a NEW EPOCH

JOSÉ PÉREZ ADÁN

CASCADE *Books* • Eugene, Oregon

MORAL SOCIOLOGY FOR A NEW EPOCH

Cascade Books
An Imprint of Wipf and Stock Publishers
199 W. 8th Ave., Suite 3
Eugene, OR 97401

www.wipfandstock.com

PAPERBACK ISBN: 979-8-3852-2797-6
HARDCOVER ISBN: 979-8-3852-2798-3
EBOOK ISBN: 979-8-3852-2799-0

Cataloguing-in-Publication data:

Names: Pérez Adán, José, author.

Title: Moral sociology for a new epoch / José Pérez Adán.

Description: Eugene, OR : Cascade Books, 2025 | Includes bibliographical references.

Identifiers: ISBN 979-8-3852-2797-6 (paperback) | ISBN 979-8-3852-2798-3 (hardcover) | ISBN 979-8-3852-2799-0 (ebook)

Subjects: LCSH: Sociology—Moral and ethical aspects.

Classification: HM216 .P45 2025 (paperback) | HM216 .P45 (ebook)

VERSION NUMBER 021425

Contents

PART 1

LET US START BY pointing out our intention to conclude this work on a positive note, advocating concrete and specific policies to improve our luck in the coming of a new era. Thus, we devote the first part of this book to what we could call the theory and the second part to what we may call the praxis. Both parts are complementary, noting that the perspective chosen in each one requires a different tone. One is more academic, and the other is more popular. We beg the reader to bear this in mind, particularly when reading these first chapters. The level of abstraction is different—a little more elevated now and more down to earth later. In any case, we have tried to avoid footnotes to make the reading easier, incorporating a few references in the text whenever necessary.

1. Introduction

WE INTRODUCE THIS FIRST part with a declaration of intentions that, at the reader's discretion, may or may not be corroborated after reading. These are issues that have been on my mind throughout my academic life, and even before, albeit in a disjointed and asystematic manner. During my formative years, most of the positions presented here were formed in a larval state, thinking against the grain. I suspect that my teachers would be surprised more than once at the difficulties of a student, otherwise hard-working and correct, to assume generalized positions and explanations. At that time, I digested disagreements by applying patience and reading while giving time to growth and maturity. In the end I find myself now presenting issues and problems that I have found initiated in the papers that I keep from those years. In one way or another the dilemma of making the character of the social subject compatible with individual freedom has occupied almost all my life; that is why I can say that this work is like the condensed summary of my academic thought. But without further ado, let's get down to business, as I want to be brief even at the cost of being dense and slow. Here are, first, my propositional intentions.

We understand by "moral sociology" the area of sociology that distinguishes the best from the worst from the point of view of social action, of the protagonism of collective subjects, and of the modes and forms of human action in social frameworks. To the extent that reflection on moral sociology proposes and assumes virtues and values to generate detectable goods through historical experience, it also forms a normative baggage that orients the valuation and understanding of the social. Thus, moral sociology explores the origins of morality in human societies, the experience of moral practices within them, and how societies can organize themselves to elaborate and propose a set of moral optimums that ensure social harmony and health. From this understanding I argue that moral sociology is a necessary academic undertaking, both from the point of view of the internal logic of

3

the social sciences and of the usefulness of this knowledge for the discernment of contents and proposals that affect life in common.

We assume at the outset that moral sociology consists of or has three main branches.

One branch, which we can call *reflexive* or *historical*, investigates broad questions such as, "What is the origin of morality?," "What is the importance of religion in social life?," "Are there timeless and universal moral precepts?," and "How can we justify that there are better and worse societies and cultures?"

Another branch of moral sociology is *descriptive*. This focuses on questions related to the results of moral experience in the lives of different collective subjects and on the particularities of the validity of certain moral creeds over time. This objective will be useful to try to offer an experiential framework with which to guide decision making by differentiating the optimal from the abysmal in collective action. To do so, it will be necessary to distinguish, first of all, value from anti-value. In the process we realize that the three most common starting approaches to assess social acts in the light of history could be called, perhaps boldly, onto-sociology (based on latent values), utilitarianism (based on consequent values), and enlightenment (based on fabricated values).

The last branch would be the *propositional* one. It concerns concrete moral issues such as those pertinent to social morality. Here we would try to solve the main moral challenges that institutions and collectives face in their daily lives, such as corruption, exclusion, human rights and duties, production and consumption systems, and moral norms and goods resulting from the emergence of new collective subjects (virtual communities and networks, iconic identities, etc.).

We believe that this is a particularly relevant topic. Moral sociology can help us to understand morality as something that shapes the backbone of the collective subject and also to distinguish moral and virtuous behaviors from immoral or vicious ones in social action and interaction. It is our intuition that in the light of this novel approach, which here and in an initiatory way we try to compose and illustrate, we can come to understand in a comprehensive way what it is that makes up the social act, what it is that lies at the core of the understanding of the human and the world we inhabit, and how we can label and qualify it for a better understanding of ourselves.

If the attempt to justify the need to argue from moral sociology for sound analysis and proposals for human behavior is satisfactory, or at least more satisfactory than the one made from other fields, we will have achieved our goal. We will be dealing with a new and incipient discipline, and it will be necessary to frame it and place it in the right place so that it can contribute both to the advancement of knowledge and to the justification of scientific endeavor. For our part, we believe it is appropriate to adopt the following starting points to develop its assumptions, objectives, scope, and methodology:

1. We do not intend to make an exercise of intrusion in fields of another owner nor to expel from ours (the social sciences) various intruders. Rather, we intend to illuminate certain areas of human behavior that have remained unfocused and almost in the dark until now, as they have been understood as the exclusive patrimony of speculative methodologies.

2. We count on God and we assume, as we will try to show below, that the most logical perspective from the social sciences is to make a discourse as if God existed, which is the proven historical experience of human societies that have succeeded each other in time, configuring the social reality in which we are immersed. We speak, therefore, of morality and not of ethics.

3. We want to mark differences with other disciplines and particularly with so-called moral philosophy, a tool that, regardless of its achievements of yesteryear, we consider not entirely adequate to understand the social reality of the human subject as it is shown to us today. Our approach starts, runs, and arrives along the broad path shaped by the irruption of sociology in the academic framework a little more than two centuries ago, with its various methodologies, discourses, and schools.

4. Finally, we hope that this contribution will also rescue social science from the abduction to which modernity has condemned it. Sociology is not the heritage of the era that is now coming to an end but rather, on the contrary, should contribute to the emergence of new cultural paradigms for the understanding of the world and its future.

To this end, we propose to develop the following topics in the first part of this work, which, as you will understand, is of a programmatic nature.

The social foundation of morality, which is where we try to give a reason for the support that allows us to speak of hierarchies setting priorities external to the thinker. Here we break a lance in defense of the relevance of the social sciences for the study of morality.

Social acts, which in our opinion make up the category of human action in the sense that they explain it and, in this process, also explain ourselves. Social action brings us together and unites us, granting us the qualification of being human and allowing us to see humanity from outside of it.

The structures of morality and virtues, the study of which allows us to make visible the social subject, still unknown to a large part of the academy. The social is neither just a circumstance nor just an object; on the contrary, in its discovery and assignment of responsibility lies the justification of any policy.

Progress and morality, where we try to involve philosophy and economics in the arguments of the text, placing their reasons in what we interpret to be their proper point. Quite distant, it seems to us, from the assumptions that are usually handled today in these disciplines.

Moral sociology as applied sociology, where we try to redirect the modern sociological narrative away from perspectives biased toward political ideology, from proposals for the exercise of power, and focus, rather, on the evaluative judgment of power itself. There are better and worse ways of behaving as humans.

The overlapping of moral sociology with other areas of knowledge, which is something, in our opinion, necessary to coordinate the different academic knowledges and undertakings in the reality of life and, more specifically, with regard to human life, in its primordial social condition. We defend that the social qualifier must be taken into account, when referring, directly or indirectly, to any inquiry about the human.

Throughout our reflection and discourse, we will not fail to refer to the central issues that have been discussed in recent years on the morality of actions and of the subjects who undertake them in the context of multidisciplinary debates; at least this is our intention at the outset. Thus, for example, the convenience (or not) of referring to moral absolutes, the typification of immorality and its public management through norms and precepts, the coexistence of religious plurality, or the typification of dichotomous spaces and spheres such as public/private, inclusion/exclusion, self/stranger, objectivity/subjectivity, and the assumption of the acceptance of alternative realities.

We ask the reader for a certain indulgence with such boldness. A new approach or paradigm is not proposed every day, and we do not consider ourselves best suited to do so. Nevertheless, we see the urgency of the task, and we do not want the social sciences to remain silent in response to the challenge that shapes the great problem of humanity in the present context, which is none other, in our opinion, than that of the confusion of opposites: good and evil, health and disease, beauty and ugliness, truth and falsehood, reality and fiction. The need for clarifying orientations that mark operative distinctions becomes peremptory. In this situation we are looking for a point of support that moves and sustains a more or less correct criterion that allows us to solve the confusion. And yes, we believe that the social sciences can offer a sure point of support for this.

> *The supposed objectivity of moral decisions appeals to the anchorage of an external authority. This is what we do when we give authority to a jury, in short, a collective, to decide whether an individual conduct can be qualified as virtuous or vicious. However, when it is a matter of hearing the case of a group conduct mediated by the action of a collective subject, the externality that should be referred to it is not easy to discern, but this does not mean there is none. The neoclassical recourse to irrationality (altruistic conduct, for example, which is free of qualification) is not enough. Beyond formalisms and cultural inertias, all human conduct can and must be examined by moral judgment. In short, morality is a mark of humanity.*

2. The Social Foundation
of Morality

IT IS SAID THAT seniority is a degree, but it is also true that it can be a hindrance if it is seen exclusively from the prism of the subject who carries it. The experience that gives the degree is not so much the age or the time that one has but the accumulation of instances that have allowed the one who has that age to understand the change of circumstances that happen in the becoming. Something that can be manifested in statements such as the following: "If I'd had the experience I have now, I would have acted differently." Certainly, realizing the weight of circumstances and contexts in decision making is what constitutes the main experiential background of each one of us. In this sense, it is true that we are children of time, so being aware of the time in which we live at any given moment is an important value when it comes to acting correctly.

This comes to mind when trying to make an accurate understanding of a certain personal life experience. It was in the early 1970s, at the beginning of the academic life of this writer. There was in the air a serious debate between determinism and freedom. On the one hand, Darwinian evolutionism and historical materialism seemed to be trying to put individual freedom in the negative. On the other hand, social Christianity unequivocally affirmed the defense of freedom and the consequent responsibility, putting in the background, if not in the back room, the conscience of collective identity. My young me, who had already opted for freedom and at the same time felt the constraint of its scarcity, boiled between secret readings to try to find a marriage between anarchism and Christianity that already then attracted him in the extreme. In this I came across a saint whose defense of freedom had captivated me and who in one of his writings affirmed the importance of collective virtue and, concretely, of humility. I must admit that I was intrigued and flattered at the same time. Well, it was my first encounter with the moral consideration of the collective subject. It was not only individuals who were responsible but also human groups.

Indeed, it took a long time to see this moral responsibility embodied in documents of higher rank and authority as far as Christianity was concerned. It is no secret for anyone who has dedicated himself to academic life to perceive that recalcitrance and stubbornness are well established in university chairs, especially in those environments where the perks that are supposed to accompany merit are considered the exclusive patrimony of feudal privileges of an ideological nature. Hence, not so long ago, some people were still tearing their clothes (and others are still tearing them now) when the last pope proclaimed a saint spoke in magisterial documents about social sin and the structures of sin. Certain so-called teachers tried to hide it and even to correct the pontiff who had dared to speak about such a delicate subject without first asking their opinion. But now this has been said and we see it as something obvious: both individual and collective subjects are susceptible to moral judgment.

What we are interested in here is collective morality, and their arguments are opposed not only by those who defend freedom against collectivism, whose ghost is still alive in some minds that still yearn for failed dictatorships, but also by other modern stubborn people, famous thinkers in vogue, who in the field of economics are called neoclassical liberals[1] or neoliberals. No wonder: ideological disputes and partisan entrenchment play a major role in academic life, particularly when it comes to morality.

Neoclassicism completely denies, as if it were a dangerous poison, the capital of the social and its configuration as a subject. Consequently, it also renounces morality, despite the fact that some of its defenders use the subterfuge of ethics to try to make a certain individual morality compatible with collective amorality. In the neoclassical camp we can find, in fact it is normal according to its majority discourse, different individuals who have different logics of choice and alternative ranges of preferences so that in no case can it be asserted which choice can be labeled as better. We are faced with an explicit relativism that excludes the assignment of value to a set of choices made based on subjective preferences. Any choice is thus justified as valid according to the internal logic chosen, thus certifying its amorality. Values are replaced here by tastes.

It is curious that it is from economics—or rather, from a specific economic theory, although it has been and in a certain way still is the predominant one—that the validity of morality in social action, here understood

1. When the author uses the terms liberal or neoliberal, he refers to their classic sense, as they are used in Europe. They refer mainly to philosophy or economics rather than politics, and they do not point to aspects of bipartisan politics.

as collective action and not only as action with social repercussions, is attempted to be violated. We will not enter the deciphering of the contradiction that in our opinion is latent in the neoclassical worldview, a task that we believe we have undertaken in other texts, but it is worth remembering that collective opinion counts for a great deal in the metaphor of the game that is at the base of the story that shapes economic neoliberalism. This is the case with the two central values in the gambling game that represents the proper functioning of the stock market mechanism: expectation and confidence, which the neoclassical creed itself understands, curiously enough, as systemic values.

Both from personal experience and from study and confrontation of opinions, we recognize how difficult it can be for a mind shaped and reinforced in the denial of the primordial character of the social to understand concepts such as structure, system, or the very expression "the social nature of the human being." We think that the difficulties emerge from a mistaken illusion in affirming, at all costs, our autonomy and our equality, as we have commented upon in *Pasar el testigo* (*Passing the Baton*, 2020). In this respect, it is necessary to remember what we did not and cannot choose: the time we were born; the family; the language; the country; the cultural, social, and religious traditions; the beliefs themselves in many cases, etc. No, the social is not the result of individual choice but, if anything, it is rather the other way around, even with the possibility of reversal *a posteriori*. We are social, we can say, before being individuals, as it is logical to think when we enter the consideration of our filial radicality. The story that individuals come first and society second is just that: a pious and sweetened neoclassical tale. We are all born into families and societies, into languages and traditions that already exist, that give us a humanity that implies, with other rights and duties, freedom.

Well, let us depart from these considerations for a moment to go hand in hand with the knowledge that can most help us to compare collective moral presuppositions, that is, history, to try to see if and how we can establish criteria of civilizational excellence. This will help us in the endeavor to discern the ambivalence of opposites. Indeed, the collaboration between history and sociology is one of the most successful among the so-called human and social sciences (as if one and the other were distinct). The so-called fathers of sociology, at least the European ones, based much of their interpretative contribution on the knowledge and pondering of history. And it can be said, at least in the opinion of yours truly, that without a broad enlightenment and understanding of historical sequences there can be no sociology or deepening of the vast field of the various so-called social sciences.

If we think of the categories that have been most used to study civilizations, we will see that we can summarize their relative weight and evaluation on the basis of moral criteria. The most studied phenomenon of collective decadence has probably been that of the decline of Roman civilization. On its remote and proximate causes, we have varied and divergent prescriptions but also significant agreements. Almost all the great contributions to the comparative study of civilizations have shed some light on Roman decadence. We see this in the work of H. G. Wells (1886–1946), Oswald Spengler (1880–1936), R. G. Collingwood (1889–1943), Christopher Dawson (1889–1970), and especially Arnold J. Toynbee (1889–1975). With the help of the father of quantitative history, the Frenchman Pierre Chaunu (1923–2009), we would like to dwell a little on the structural causes of decadence in the comparative study of cultures and civilizations, which we believe to be very pertinent to the subject we are trying to present.

First, allow me to quote one of the most distinguished minds of humanity, St. Augustine of Hippo, for whom the cause of Roman decadence lies in injustice. An unjust state could not endure despite the virtues that had contributed to its rise. Could Augustine not, we wonder, say the same of Western culture today? Could he not say of us that the cause of our decline is the injustice that shapes us, an injustice that causes inequality to grow among us and excludes many from the right to life? Certainly, the parallels between Roman decadence and the decadence of so-called Western civilization, insofar as we circumscribe it to the historical period we have come to call modernity, are numerous.

For those great prototypes of the virtue on which Rome was built, Cato and Cicero, Roman identity was intrinsically linked to the free assertion of the collective over the personal. When Sallust puts in Cato's mouth the denunciation of the corruptions that were undermining the republican virtues, he sentences: "Publice egestatem, privatim opulentiam" (the misery of the public and the opulence of the private). The great heroes of the first Rome, Cincinnatus, Camillo, and Regulus, were shown as examples of what we can call "the public affluence and the private sobriety," that is in definitive a defense freely assumed of the primacy of the collective thing on the personal thing. In this we can detect, as do most of the authors mentioned, a virtuous behavior that denotes a high degree of moral quality.

Chaunu, in his masterful work *History and Decadence*, published in Spanish in 1983, states that it is our ineptitude to ensure the ability to live beyond one's own self that is the greatest obstacle to our collective survival: we cannot, he says, pronounce a discourse that ensures the minimum coherence necessary to the will to live of societies irreversibly formed more and more by individual consciences tragically isolated in the interrogation of a destiny irreversibly separated from other destinies. The contrast between the transpersonal one and the transpersonal all puts the finger on the sore spot of the scourge of individualism.

Chaunu's work is prophetic, erudite, and very current. We share his intuition that what really counts when measuring and comparing both progress and decadence is an equation that we could describe as follows: the amount of happiness plus the amount of life divided by the amount of unhappiness plus the amount of lives lost. Chaunu points out as a signaling symptom of the crisis of contemporary civilization the lack of respect for human life and the fact that it is seen as reasonable that some put the life of others in function of their own and not the other way around, their own life in function of others. The review of history and the work of the French historian is very exhaustive and complete in this respect; it also gives us this lesson: selfishness and individualism are the recipe for failure. On the other hand, civilizational success is always accompanied by differentiated, free, and benevolent cooperation beyond one and beyond the present time. Thus, for Chaunu, the image of this necessary characteristic for the progress and advancement of civilization is something as communitarian as the family open to children.

The most important of cultural historians, the Englishman Arnold Toynbee, was of a similar opinion. Toynbee understood cooperation as the sum of creativity and mimesis, and its absence certified the consequent loss of social unity in a human group that was beginning to cease to be a whole. In his monumental *A Study of History*, published in eleven volumes from 1934 to 1961, Toynbee asserted that nemesis or the exhaustion of creativity is a consequence of the idolization of an ephemeral self that goes hand in hand with the lack of common purpose and the ideal of collective life.

Human decadence in history throughout cultures and civilizations has many causes, but if, according to the academic literature and the authors mentioned above, we had to point out only one, it would be the loss of moral quality and of binding moral referents. This is also, in my opinion, the most important problem we have as a society today.

But if we talk about civilization, cultures, and moral quality, we obviously have in mind a reference point that cannot be internal to any of them, because in that case we would not be able to compare them, to evaluate them, or to separate one of them to compare it with itself over time through a process of change. We have in mind a series of values that we can label as general or common that we can standardize to apply them to different peoples, groups, and cultures and also to the historical validity of one of these collective units. And this is where God comes in.

Without recourse to God, the neutrality that can be demanded of introspection and the evaluative extrapolation of human groups is not possible, nor is it possible to aspire to any kind of evaluative objectivity that goes beyond the momentary circumstance or the mind of an individual, which is the case we are dealing with here in comparing civilizations. Based on what conceptual parameters could we proclaim and use values that we label as social and valid in a general and timeless way without a higher than human foundation? Reason discovers that we cannot adequately reason about the synchronic and diachronic human whole without appealing to God. On the one hand, without a universal foundation, we cannot make universal judgments, and on the other hand, only an unconditioned one can unconditionally compel. As seems to be a general agreement among both those who see its necessity and those who do not, without God everything is relative and moral discourse collapses in an instantaneousness that, in my opinion, puts some who have power and legitimacy at the mercy of others who lack it.

But if one goes to the historical experience, one finds that indeed the recognition of God has been and is an almost universal resource. It is what has sanctioned moral conduct in practically all societies, although reason and the examination of certain situations tell us that the logical processes by which in many instances the hierarchy of conduct between moral and immoral has been arrived at has been vitiated from the beginning by attributing to God a justification that is impossible even for God himself. They are the moments and circumstances in which the constituted human powers have tried to use God to their benefit to sanction the exploitation or extermination of the labeled as other (we will insist on this later). In any case, if we review the collective subject in its development throughout history, we observe an analogous disposition with respect to the recourse to God. The opinion is almost unanimous, although it may be surprising in certain environments of aristocratic bias or nostalgia, as are some of the positions of the roots established in a large part of the academic world. It must be remembered that the normal human being is to believe in God, and this is so both diachronically and synchronically. Diachronically because anthropology and history say so. The normal thing in almost all cultures, in all human history, has been to believe in God. We could say that human beings are naturally religious and believers, and history tells us that. Synchronically, on the other hand, because it is also so today: most of humanity believes in God. From this we can infer that it is normal for human beings to believe in God.

It is not hidden from us that there are colleagues who, without denying this evidence, put it in parentheses, qualifying it as barbarism, primitivism, magical illusionism, or even collective alienation, and it may seem strange to some that a more or less academic book like this one pronounces itself so clearly in this way and from the beginning in this regard. We think that the astonishment, if it occurs, may be due in a certain way, particularly in those academic environments, to a strong and scarce recourse to self-criticism. The supposedly enlightened position in the discourse of the social sciences that denies God, sometimes in an imperative way, is difficult to accept, and we can point out at least two contradictions that arise from the denialist premises themselves. One of the contradictions stands out when we note the implicit defense made by the negationist, who often thinks he is advanced with respect to ordinary mortals, of unidirectional progress understood as a necessary *a priori* in the succession of generations and of which his own assumptions would form part, something that has been disproved by recent history, which shows evident signs of decadence. The optimism of the end of history theory has been replaced by the pessimism of the end of modernity. A pessimism that in some instances goes beyond the supposed end of the civilizational or cultural cycle by pointing out features and risks of cataclysmic implosion in the latent atomic danger, the always fearsome research in chemical and biological weapons, or the challenges implicit in environmental sustainability. There is here in the negationist position a form of unfounded idealism with strong doses of historical determinism and to which we will also return later. The other contradiction is based on the difficulties these positions encounter in trying to reconcile the defense of the democratic ethos with the rejection of positions so widely and ardently defended by a substantive and plural majority of humanity. It is not surprising in this sense to find a certain aristocratic haughtiness residing in many negationist academics. The atheist militancy of certain figures in the academic world cannot be surprising, even though it is a minority, as noted by Philip Jenkins in *The Next Christendom: The Coming of Global Christianity* (2002) and *The New Anti-Catholicism* (2005) and Rodney Stark in *The Victory of Reason* (2005), among others.

On the other hand, the recourse to the divine can also be found in the investigative intention of social science from its beginnings. Without going any further, let us look briefly at the initiators of the academic establishment of sociology in Europe, Émile Durkheim (1858–1917) and Max Weber (1864–1920). The original text of *The Elementary Forms of Religious Life* dates from 1912, and there Durkheim affirms that the consideration of the sacred is inscribed in man while defending as the objective of the discipline the understanding and the needs that derive from this fact, which forms an inseparable part of the human experience. For the Frenchman, the religious nature of man is an essential and permanent aspect of humanity and is linked to morality; hence, explaining morality in a rational way is a permanent challenge for the social sciences, which is equivalent in a certain way to establishing solid links with theology. The social sciences do not try to investigate the what and the who of God but how it affects us through morality. In fact, Durkheim never stopped thinking about morality, and his ideas on the subject are present and evolved throughout his work, leaving unfinished, or rather only sketched, the beginning of what was supposed to be his recapitulation on the subject, the text *Morale*.

In the case of Weber, both in *The Protestant Ethic and the Spirit of Capitalism* (1905) and in *Economy and Society* (1922), he sees the religious imprint transformed through processes of rationalization into operative guidelines for action of a normative character imbued in bureaucracies that draw and propose moral codes. The danger lies in the loss of meaning that would produce a rupture in the continuum that goes from the religious superstructure to the bureaucratic structure and the infrastructure of action that would deprive vital operational issues, mostly those of an economic nature, of rational justification. Thus, a relationship could be established between secularization and materialism, which would detract from moral quality or distort the process of consolidation of the functioning of the so-called capitalist economy, for example, with the disappearance of savings.

We see, with all this, that God is a social issue. We mean to say that while on a personal level it may not be a relevant issue, and in fact it is not for many, on a social level it always is. Human relationships are based on a shared morality, and there is no moral environment that can withstand the denial of God in the long run. In God is the ultimate, if distant, foundation of morality.

Amitai Etzioni (1929–2023), in his seminal *The Moral Dimension* (1988), brings central ideas to the theme, present in all his work, which denotes a harmony between sociological work, reciprocal and responsible commitment, and respect for the transcendent. For the late Georgetown professor, a moral act fulfills four criteria: it follows some kind of imperative that we can understand as duty, which we distinguish from pleasure and which goes beyond the instrumental reason that applies the analysis of the cost-benefit ratio; it is in some way generalizable through the reasoning of the golden rule: act and treat as you wish others to act and treat you; it is symmetrical in the sense that it grants others who share circumstances the same right; and it is intrinsically motivated by expressing a kind of commitment outside the analysis of means and ends. In other words, for Etzioni the implicit acceptance of morality somehow precedes, even only from the logical perspective, the moral act itself.

There is here, as it were, a link between transcendence and immanence, which presupposes their relationship and which is better explained in the consideration of collective subjects than in the individual subject. I was not at all surprised when, in one of our periodic conversations prior to his death, J. V. Marqués, my sociology department colleague and recognized guru of the radical and supposedly atheist left in the city, confessed to me that he was a Christian and argued this by saying that he was morally and culturally Christian if not personally so. Days later, he wrote an article in his regular column entitled "I Am a Christian" that shocked more than one person. In that conversation, Marqués acknowledged to me that morality was outside of us—that is why we could share it and relate to each other, otherwise it was not morality but interest—and that he believed in God intellectually (specifically the Christian God, who was the most rational), although he did not like the church. I tell this because I have often encountered my colleague's position in certain environments, and I think that the reader may have experienced the same thing. Indeed, outside of God, it is very difficult to sustain the social. History shows us several failed experiences, some of them recent and very painful, but one thinks that they are due, in great part, despite their majority following in some intellectual environments, to a previous lack of discursive reason.

Perhaps because of all this, one can only explain the acceptance of that medieval dictum trying to lay the foundations of the harmonious functioning of a society on the basis of a law "as if God did not exist" in the ignorance of the social. It would have been a different story if what appeared two hundred years ago, with the full recognition of the social sciences in academic life, had happened earlier. Although it is true that everything has its course, we are now in a position to argue moral reasoning in a different way and combining premises that did not exist in the past.

That is why Slavoj Žižek's objection to Ivan Karamazov seems to us cheap and weak. The Slovenian philosopher says that if God exists, everything is permitted (in his name), while Dostoevsky's character did not refer to specific moral or immoral acts but to the principle of morality. What God says is different from whether he exists. Moral sociology, nor of course Žižek (although we believe he would like to), cannot go into what God says or does not say, or at least cannot go into it before seeing that it exists and the latter suffices, for the moment, to substantiate the existence of a morality. To unravel the contents of that morality we will have to turn to other areas of knowledge, in our opinion mainly history and theology, and with them and in the meantime continue with our propositional inquiry on moral sociology.

Far from all relativism, the human act as a social act can be analyzed as a guarantor of existence. There are the we with whom we are a who. The distinction so often made between society and nature is blurred by subscribing to the social conception of nature. The existences can be recognized and by recognizing each other, can be compared, and hence we can aspire to be better, as individuals, as families, as societies, or as earthlings.

3. Social Acts

MUCH OF CLASSICAL MORALITY considers that there is only one moral subject, the human being, who is usually understood as the individual subject, and assumes that his end is happiness or, to put it in Aristotelian terms, *eudaimonia*. This is very short and scarce, if not completely wrong. In our analysis, since here we start from the assumption that collective subjects are also, insofar as they perform social acts, subjects of morality, we must also ask ourselves two recurring questions that, regardless of the fact that they may not have an answer, we cannot fail to ask: what is the end of society as such and of human collectives in general, and can we speak of two types of moral acts in individual subjects, some internal to them without social repercussions and others that are social acts? On the other hand, we need to elucidate what moral goods are beyond the exercise of the virtues that we will talk about later and ask ourselves if there is some kind of common moral sense that encompasses all types of subjects capable of performing social acts akin to what the ancients called synderesis. But let us go by parts.

First, we will leave aside onto- or meta-social questions that we intend to deal with in the last chapter of this first part, and we will stop here to note that, unlike what may be thought or discussed about other subjects, society has neither nature nor essence, and that the very idea of distinguishing between nature and society is a gratuitous daring that today cannot be done lightly. Rather, we will have to consider and bear in mind the social character of nature insofar as the distinction between reason and unreason necessarily involves humanity in its (nature's) survival. We will use the environment as a framework for reflection to illustrate our point.

The attempt to rationalize nature has yielded a multitude of categorizations throughout the history of science. The naturalists of the eighteenth century, especially the Swede Carl Linnaeus, elevated the categorization of the animate world to an autonomous branch of knowledge under the name of taxonomy. It must be recognized that Linnaeus did a brilliant job that has kept many students of biological sciences busy and amused during all these years. Linnaeus's classification is now outdated. In recent years new kingdoms of life have been described in addition to plant and animal.

Physicists have also succumbed to the classificatory design. They do not speak of nature but of matter, thus including parts discarded by biologists such as inert matter. Their classification ranges from elementary particles to the society of societies.

Today we know that neither matter nor nature has designs alien to the one who thinks it. And not because we build (or destroy) nature from within it, something to which we would have nothing to object because it would be a law, pattern, or "natural" evolution, but because the world of external objects and subjects is not thinkable (by us) in an autonomous way, although it can exist (without us) in that way. That is to say, nature is not alien to us, not because human society is nature, but because nature, after its manipulation by us, is society. Indeed, nature is today in a certain way our prisoner because we think that we can finish with it and destroy it. It is in this sense that we can consider the history of sociology as a story of animated pirates in search of hidden treasure. The search was indeed fruitful, but it yielded a paradoxical find: the treasure sought was the physical nature of the social world (Comte) and the lucky find has been the social nature of the physical world, so to speak.

The old notion of natural laws must therefore be seen as a generalization which, although it has been useful in the past, does not place us in the present in a position to understand ourselves, no longer as victims but as guardians of nature. We say this in the healthy understanding that perhaps the only thing to which the ancient concept of natural law, with its dimensions of universality and immutability, can be rigorously applied is the unity in the sense of mutual and continuous dependence of all that exists in and through time. That is why the taxonomies and divisions of matter that we may make are not to be understood as exhaustive, universal, and permanent. What makes us human remains, regardless of whether our human actions may occasionally deviate from our humanity. Human progress, in this sense, is not the improvement of what is constitutive in our individual humanities, something that is given to us, but the progress of our human society, which is perfectible and encompasses both the relationship between us and the relationship between us and the environment. It is certainly the lack of scientific humility that led from simplification to universalization and from there to the cataloguing of nature and creation in general, as better or worse, perfect or imperfect. For taxonomy, in Linnaeus's time, the passage of time was not important because the laws of the divisions were fixed, and it was assumed that our situation of helpless dependence on the environment was also fixed. Now, however, the passage of time is the most important thing because we know that it has substantially changed our understanding of the world. We used to think that nature could destroy mankind, but relatively recently we have become aware that mankind can destroy nature and consequently destroy all.

What has happened, among other cosmological appreciations that can and ought to be made, is that we have gone from a mostly biospheric conception of life to a noospheric one, as we were told by Vladimir Vernadsky (1863–1945), for whom reason was a cosmic and geological force. Reason, as a primordial concept, distinguishes itself here from nature, to relate to it and become involved in it.

When we ask ourselves about the nature of (physical) nature, we observe that since the preservation of the environment has come to be perceived as an illusory and difficult-to-guarantee good, the criteria of rationalization about the very goodness of historical continuity have taken a revolutionary turn. If this is going to end with the threat of an ecological holocaust, individualism arises, what does it matter when it is, if it will be after I am finished? In other words, is there any moral reason why historical continuity is better than discontinuity as long as the latter is not directly procured as an attack on the discretion of others?

What we are ultimately asking with these questions is the dilemma as to whether the environment is a good in itself or a good for someone. If the environment is a good in itself, which happens to be, in addition, a conditioning factor for life and, therefore, for historical continuity, it seems clear that discontinuity, the end of the world, or ecological holocaust should be considered as a dysfunction in all cases and assumptions. This, which seems to be the majority opinion in contemporary society (the dysfunctionality of death, both individual and collective, is widely assumed), clashes, however, with one of the very cultural presuppositions of the Western world. Indeed, for Christianity, the end of the world, like its beginning, are functional elements contemplated as positive by the messianic eschatology itself.

On the contrary, if the environment is a good for someone, discontinuity need not always be seen as dysfunctional. The problem posed by this position is that of elucidating the responsibilities of that someone toward nature. In other words, what is the power of "someone" in his or her relationship with the environment and what are its limits? Can we discover the owners of the natural environment, in the sense of those who effectively and legitimately have power and responsibility over it? The answer to this question lies in discovering "someone": the reference for whom the environment is a good.

Our position is that the natural environment is always a good for all of us. That is, "someone" is us—all of us—always. Us, because the physical world is our prey: it is at the whim of thinkers, for better or for worse. All, because the unity of the environment collectivizes society. We are all the North and the South, the rich and the poor, the black and the white. In our interconnected and globalized world there is no room for selective and independent appropriations of the natural environment by sectorial differentiated collectives. And always because the physical world erases time. To that someone belong both the rational animals who have been and those who will be. The environment belongs to those, as well as to these, as well as to those of us who are now, who coincide in time (or in its absence) through the actions of deferred effect and those carried out by those social subjects (towns, families, etc.) whose life transcends that of their members.

Therefore, if the environment is a good for us all, always, the right and property over nature belongs to a diachronic universal social collective, which can only be disintegrated by usurpation. The capacity of usurpation, however, can be singularized in time and space by those who can make unquestionable decisions by arrogating illegitimate power to themselves. Therefore, environmental deterioration, when produced by inconsiderate actions toward the spatial and diachronic all, results in usurpation by those who exercise power in time through actions or omissions of deferred effect that affect another time or space. This is why individualism and the liberalism that protects it entail usurpation when we consider the ecological crisis. It is its antisocial ethos that makes individualism reprehensible, and not only its manifest iniquity against the natural environment, although the manifest environmental deterioration around us is what motivates us to raise these considerations. That is why we believe that recognizing the social character of nature is nowadays an indispensable and peremptory condition to think ourselves capable of continuing it.

We can label this position as eco-rationalist. Environmental problems give us a protagonism that marks the recognition of concrete responsibilities. And particularly the responsibility to care for, protect, and conserve the environment. In this sense, humans are not just another species, and if we are capable of destroying, we are also capable of improving. The basic distinction in this case is that between reason and unreason rather than the supposed opposition that some have claimed to see between reason and nature. On the contrary, both reason and nature are on the same side, and both can be described as social.

At this point we can see that from every social act, whether in its origin or in its repercussions, emanates a moral evaluation. We are in a world that has not been created by us, and whatever the rules, dimensions, or mandates may or may not be constitutive of the creator, of God, we will have to try to discover their meaning to interpret our life in an adequate way. We do not consider whether there is morality beyond social acts; in any case, it is not the subject of our discipline. But as far as our relationships are concerned, the goods given by those who have preceded us, and that have been received by us as such, condition our actions to the extent that our finitude inevitably implies that we, too, become givers of a legacy. On the one hand, our dia-chronic condition, whether we want it or not, imputes responsibilities to us. On the other hand, our social condition, insofar as it implies a relationship with someone else, does too.

From the questions we posed at the beginning of this chapter and after the arguments put forward so far, we can keep the importance of the change of pronouns. On the purpose of the social we are now looking for a who rather than a what. Thus, we see it plausible to distinguish between the tran-scendent who (God) and the social who, where the idea of the we-all and we-always disposed us to think about the functionality of the different so-cieties with respect to the human whole in an analogous way to how we can understand the function of individual and collective subjects with respect to the social categories to which their belonging refers: individuals in families or families in society. As to whether we can speak of two types of morality according to the social nature or not of the act in question, moral sociology can only deal with the morality of social acts and leaves the field open so that if other areas of knowledge decide to unravel the morality derived from nonsocial actions they can do so without any qualms.

On moral goods we also focus on the importance of who, in this case to whom the social action carried out by a subject brings a good. Here synderesis would lead us to see the moral sense in the spheres or social environments to which the social act gives meaning, gives health, gives improvement.

As to whether this can be called a morality of care akin to what some philosophers such as Annette Baier (1929–2012) called the ethics of care, we will say that we are moving in another direction. We understand the social act as an act of service and, in this sense, it would be possible to label our argument as that of a servant morality (pro quem), but we believe that it is better to speak simply of understanding synderesis as having sufficient social sense (it can be read as conscience) to act and judge correctly, ratio-nally well, under the gaze of God. Thus, under the prism of moral optimiza-tion we can say that social acts establish a connection between servants and served that results in social improvement.

Before proceeding further, it would be convenient to make a brief ref-erence to the relationship between social acts, public goods, and common goods, since this is a terminology in use in the academic literature today. Public goods, according to Paul Samuelson (1915–2009), are those that can be used by many subjects without diminishing their availability to others; they are both tangible goods, such as infrastructures for common use, and traditions of good citizenship, which were called into question some time ago when they were considered as a utility susceptible to maximization. Common goods, according to Elinor Ostrom (1933–2012), are shared resources (forests, water, fishing, etc.) susceptible to regulation and which were more recently called into question by being considered a matter for administrative rather than communal decision. The dilemma often raised here is whether service can be considered as a form of self-interest beyond management issues such as efficiency and effectiveness. In both cases both Samuelson and Ostrom considered that the market was not the optimal place to ventilate the regulation of public and common goods and that they could neither be subjected to privacy criteria nor to bureaucratic criteria unrelated to the condition of the subjects involved in their maintenance and use. To this end, it became more or less clear that the typical neoclassical binary public/private distinction did not meet the minimum criteria for understanding the problems arising from the conceptualization of these goods.

On the contrary, a third Nobel laureate in economics, James Buchanan (1919–2013), argued in his theory of public choice that the use of public and common goods is also subject to the mono-utility of self-interest and that the best way to defend these goods as goods is either to understand selfishness as a good or altruism as an irrational attitude, as an exception not subject to consideration. Here not all social acts are susceptible to be subjected to a criterion of morality, and it would be better to leave morality out of the sphere of relation of acts with goods as public intrusion is left out of the private. Does the morality that is supposed to motivate service fit or not in the benefit that is expected from an action that implies assuming a cost?

In examining the relationship between collective action and free uses, Ostrom showed that the subjects involved tend to cooperate rather than confront each other, long before threats of sustainability or scarcity arise, and when there are guarantees that they will not arise. This is what Amitai Etzioni called, referring to the prisoner's dilemma, the cooperative prisoner in doubting whether self-interest is beneficial beyond and before examining whether it contributes to a public good. In short, Etzioni also showed that it is by no means clear that moral factors should be dissociated from social acts and concluded that their mutual intertwining gives meaning, both explanatory and predictive, to action. The founder of socioeconomics here takes the side of Ostrom and Samuelson in excluding the mono-utility of economic interpretation as advocated by Buchanan. But this does not in itself explain the good of altruistic rationality as opposed to another rationality that we can call instrumental. In fact, Buchanan also defends morality outside the market by assuming the well-known public/private binary perspective. If we acknowledge that moral values are important to our economic well-being, it follows that we must all "pay the preacher"; to do good benefits us. In other words, ethics always pays.

Etzioni closes, in our opinion correctly, the debate speaking of the irreducibility of moral conduct: it is not reducible to mercantile criteria. The persistence of public and common goods as goods is both proof and example that social action must also be examined morally as a whole. And this contrasts with certain interpretations of the concept of mercantile good that argue the notion that subjects behave morally only as long as it makes sense from the economic point of view. It seems that both factors, moral and economic, are involved in the action regardless of whether it can be realized and bring cases of subjects who act solely moved by interest (the most today) as well as of subjects moved solely by morality (the least today). Thus, it is appropriate to consider human choices as events in which interest and morality are always involved and combined in a complex and to some extent indescribable way. To reduce the categories of service and profit to the same thing is a mistake, however much they may cooperate on certain occasions. As widespread as relativism is today, the opposites must remain distinct.

The mercantile actions to which we have just referred when dealing with certain economic goods are so of both individual and collective subjects. We do not distinguish between an individual and a collective rationality in the supposition that some of them are not under the scope of both moral criteria and instrumental criteria. Collective action, organized or not, does not presuppose a necessary diminution of the criteria of efficacy and efficiency compared to other types of action. Nor can it be said that amoral or immoral action ordinarily has competitive advantages in the market or in a system governed exclusively by instrumental criteria. The differences, if any or if they are brought to the case, should be sought in the different types of collectivities. It may be interpreted as evident that collectivities with a high degree of consensus on the goals and objectives to be pursued are more efficient in making decisions in this regard than collectivities with high levels of dissent and internal conflict. But let us not equate efficiency with morality. As we shall see below, the relationship between social acts and morality is not only of ends but also of means (if this moral distinction can be made) and morality is not only of actions but also of subjects who are supposed to have the capacity to make a prior moral choice between different attitudes, values, and principles.

As we see, the consideration of the morality of the social act understood in a non-reductive way adds complexity to the evaluative interpretation of any type of action. But this should not, for the sake of simplicity or explanatory simplicity, reduce the approach to moral judgment. One remembers in his youth the strong impression caused by seeing for the first time on the black and white television of that era the representation of what for many is F. Lope de Vega's masterpiece, *Fuenteovejuna* (1613), and the shocking memory of the end of the Comendador: *Saqueáronle la casa / Cual si de enemigos fuese / Y gozosos, entre todos / Han repartido sus bienes* ("They looted his house / As if they were enemies / And rejoicing, among all / They have distributed his goods"). The play has a new character, the collective, which replaces the traditional tragic hero. In the words of Menéndez y Pelayo, there is no individual protagonist; there is no hero other than the demos, the council of Fuenteovejuna. And that protagonist faces a moral judgment that in the play ends up winning. It is a complex subject, certainly, beyond literary study, but it must be approached from all its angles.

We propose here to give reasons for the study of morality from the perspective of the social sciences and specifically of sociology. Moral sociology puts social acts where other disciplines put the so-called human acts, to discern the matter of moral reflection. A reflection that can be done in many ways even within the same area of knowledge. As we said at the beginning, we hope that this initial proposal that we make now generates enough thought so that these various other reflections can be accommodated within what we call here moral sociology.

> *The structures of virtue shape the excellence of a society or of any of us. The uses and customs, and the culture, beliefs, traditions, and laws that protect and promote them in the different spheres of relationship are of great importance here.*

4. Morality, Structures, and Virtues

IN SOCIOLOGY TEXTBOOKS, A chapter is usually reserved for social structure. Generally, the discourse refers to the network of social conventions and institutions that, in an organized and more or less legitimate and accepted way make up the skeleton of a society. Here we are interested in seeing that social structures are sustained by living organizations that, under the protection of public or private, legal or illegal undertakings, seek functional or dysfunctional aspects that shape the virtues or defects of a human group. Almost always the chapter on social structure in these textbooks is one of the most complex of the subject in question and a good teacher will resort to examples to smooth and facilitate the understanding of the students. Not that this is a lesson or that it is necessary to explain the difference between structure, superstructure, and infrastructure, but it is also worth going to the examples to better explain ourselves and get to where we want to go.

We have already mentioned, without naming him, St. John Paul II when, in his encyclical *Sollicitudo Rei Socialis* (1987), he spoke of the structures of sin. In this text we will first refer to structures of evil that configure assumed and valid patterns in time, shaped around a nucleus of opinion, a custom or usage, or even a constituted power, that generate one or several evils with results of disruption, dysfunctionality, abuse, and the proliferation of victims.

We will now put together a list of structures of evil and their main added vice or vices which, being present in our societies, we hope will be sufficiently graphic to point out their inappropriateness. Keep in mind that we use this discourse to provide us with explanatory resources that can later help us to compare and label something, specifically one social experience, as better than another. Thus, we turn first to organizations with victimizing means or ends, such as the underworld or the cartel. In both cases we find solid social structures that survive attempts at extinction even by powerful states. The vices that we can link to these structures are crimes of blood, force, and addiction to harmful substances. To point out another example, we can go to a more abstract level of operation when we bring up the structures and patterns that support trafficking or the unnatural marriage of political power and profit. Here we would highlight the associated vices of prostitution and corruption. We can still go up the level of abstraction to look at assumed cultures that have behind them the thrust of various agents with concerted interests shaping "fashions" that impel follow-up. Here we would situate the structures of consumerism, hedonism, and the commodification of life, with the vices derived from alienation and the destruction of the environment for the first, from anomie and asocial self-absorption for the second, and from the culture of discarding and the reification of the other for the third. We can also refer to structures of evil that are centered on the hook of a single gadget that proves to be victimizing, such as a punctual and generalized addiction, that generates a main vice, such as selfishness for screen addiction, if it is the case.

With these examples we wanted to show the moral weight that social structures can have and the correspondence between evil structures in their different degrees of concreteness and visibility and victims suffering from specific vices. But perhaps where the importance of deepening the study of moral sociology can be seen more clearly is in the link that we can establish between structures of virtue and concrete virtues, since here we do have a positive objective of social excellence that will be convenient to pursue as an achievement.

As we are going to be more prolix, even without pretending to be exhaustive, in the enumeration of both the structures of virtue and the concrete virtues, it will be convenient to dwell first on one and then on the other with the implicit object of outlining above the structural character of some and below the social reason of the others. Thus, when we refer to the structures, we will always have in mind the collective subject that carries them, while when we refer to the virtues, we cannot forget that we point out the virtues-bridge that communicates the individual subject with the collective.

The structures of virtue are both the configuration of social customs and the organizations and organized collectives that permeate the mood and group culture. They are present not only in the collective actions of societies and groups but also with the acquiescence of the individual subject in his feelings, actions, and opinions. The structures of virtue facilitate the virtuous exercise of individual and collective action, and in the same way that the structures of evil facilitate the production of evils and damages, the structures of virtue do so with goods and goodness. There is no determination that violates freedoms in either case, but there is a weight and one that can come to have identity characteristics and, in this sense, suppose a positive or negative conditioning for the morality of the action or of the subject that undertakes it.

If we refer to organized structures in the same way as we referred to the underworld or the cartel, here we can point to those organizations within specific areas of operation (such as those promoting development, justice, and solidarity; charitable-religious organizations; or recreational-sports and artistic organizations) that have as their objective and trajectory the attainment of social goods with means related to the goodness of the objectives. On the other hand, if we refer to nonorganized structures, we will note those that denote shared values that become visible in the appreciation they enjoy and in the incorporation into the tradition that configures each society of an identity that can be appreciated and distinguished from outside it. In one case, we will have institutions such as churches, the orderly and fair market, or mechanisms of participation or, on the contrary, of respect for non-participation. In another case, we will have customs such as civility, mutual trust, recognition of others, thrift, service, industriousness, or responsible subsidiarity. Still from another approach, we will have generalized and assumed defenses such as that of fame, privacy, human rights and duties, creativity, or criticism. And lastly, from another point of view, we will have loves concretized in facts such as family, silence, tranquility, science, tradition, or gratuitousness. These are examples of the weight that a society may have given in a continuous and sustained way over time to a trace or aspect of the value universe until it becomes a sign of identity in ways of doing and understanding life in common until it becomes part of the conformation of its distinctive peculiarity as a consolidated structure of operability.

These structures of virtue and others that we could discover and outline may be present or not and in varying degrees randomly in different societies and human environments. The excellence of the life of a community depends largely on the number and quality of its structures of virtue, and it will be good that the conscience and conformation of belonging to a human group carries with it the idea of promoting and rooting in its bosom the structures of virtue that its idiosyncrasy advises. Thus, we think that if a wise and plausible objective for many governments is to become unnecessary in the long run, this can only be achieved to the extent that they can be replaced by the minimum of structures of virtue that the circumstances and potentialities of their existence make necessary.

If we refer now to the virtues, we have noted before virtues-bridge, that they come from one to the social directly and not indirectly. In many cases, they come from the prevalence in a given environment and surroundings of social structures that condition or promote them. Virtue, according to the classical definition, is a good operative habit, but the virtues to which we now refer are those that do good outside of oneself. A good that we understand as social good insofar as it has its direct effect on society: a good *to whom* (bonus *ad quem*). Thus, from among the great number of aspects that we can consider when understanding and proposing virtues, three main groups can be identified from a didactic point of view. We can consider those that refer to or correspond to calls of social interpellation such as respect, solidarity, mutual help, exemplarity, or the defense of others. They can also refer to sought-after and incorporated habits that facilitate the call to live and contribute to a dignified and healthy social life, such as the capacity for self-management, cleanliness and hygiene, religiosity, culture, security, or order. And they can also be understood as objectives of collective perfection that depend on or pass through one's own participation, such as love of freedom, plurality, nature, equity, hospitality, festivity, art, piety, or the good use and care of words. These are virtues that do not have their primary end in oneself but that make one better in the understanding that if one is not better for others, perhaps one cannot be better for oneself either.

Some authors, such as Hans Jonas (*Principle of Responsibility*, 1979), Alasdair MacIntyre (*Dependent Rational Animals*, 2001), and the previously mentioned Etzioni, can agree with many of the approaches presented here. Particularly MacIntyre, who highly values the historical and teleological, not to say narrative, sense of the evolution of ideas in the conformation of rational traditions that explain the understanding of human action, is right, as is Etzioni by another route, in seeing society as a learning community that provides interpretative criteria for moral orientation by distinguishing virtue from vice. We must not discard from this historical interpretation the understanding that we can make of the relationship between creator and creature, between God and us, that may have occurred in the course of the historical time to which we are subject. In these stories that make up collective memory, we have at our disposal stories and experiences that give rise to interpretation and the consequent formation of canons of excellence about what it means to do good. Javier Gomá (*Tetralogía de la ejemplaridad*, 2010) has also addressed the issue. It is necessary, however, to emphasize that the action that shapes historical experience involves a constitutive plurality of subjects that cannot be assimilated abstractly, so we must always bear in mind the collective subjects in their formal and constitutive variety. Hence the importance of giving the prominence they deserve to the structures of virtue that vertebrate these subjects without which any attempt to make and understand progress is futile.

A curious question now arises: how do we propose virtue? In this regard, and again with apologies to my own experience, I can say that one has detected three main stages in one's life in the order of things that we are describing. There was a first one back in late childhood and early youth that I can call epic in which I felt immersed in the sociology of the feat. At first through comic books, which attracted my childish curiosity, and my admiration for drawing and for characters generally secondary at the shadow of such Spanish comic heroes as *Capitán Trueno*, *Jabato*, or the good German that, due to its rarity, had to be searched with a magnifying glass between the war exploits while reading a story of *Hazañas Bélicas*. Later, already in the awakening of the incipient intellectual curiosity that the first books gave me, the attraction went with the Hispanic epic annexed to the discovery of America and with the lives of saints. Then came, from my first years of university, although it was already incipient some time before, a long period of sociology that I call rejection, with an awakening of criticism that turned into a deep repudiation of the vice that I detected everywhere: a haughty, liberticidal, and iconoclastic world where dogmatism, ugliness, and militant materialism seemed to triumph; a world from which I wanted to leave without knowing where to go. Finally, a third stage was established, also long, of sociology that I can label receptive, which combined two aspects, one passive and fun, using the term rightly coined by Juan Carlos Barajas, in which, with a permanent reservation in the viewpoint of the main square, one was ready to observe the passage of people and assume their desires and needs, and another active, involved, and committed, using the term by Etzioni, which militated, or tried to do so, in helping those needs.

It follows that the best recipe that occurs to this writer to propose virtue is to try to incarnate it, even if one never succeeds in doing so. Discernment implies, in our opinion, necessarily the course. I mean that I understand that it is not enough, as the classics and their followers affirm (it is curious how long the text proposed to Nicomacheus has been in force, as if the world had not changed since then) to have a clear bifrontal purpose (eudaemonistic and teleological). One understands that a virtuous morality must focus on doing, on walking in oneself, and no longer only on knowing where the natural goal is (supposedly but not with certainty in happiness) and the supernatural one (in salvation). Not only do we have to go the right way and in the right direction, of which we may never be sure, but we ought to walk well.

The good Aristotle said that the proper purpose of the human being was contemplation. He might as well have said something else and moved on in view of the lack of criticism employed by his followers in this. It is not that I think it is wrong, it is just that it is not entirely justified, although one senses that in a slave society it might be logical for the Hellenist to think this way (badly, I add). What if he had said that the proper purpose of the human being was to work well, or to live well together, or to love God and neighbor? One understands that he would have been much more correct and more solidly based on a walking morality.

It is true that the Hellenist corrected the Socratic moral intellectualism that equated virtue with knowledge, but it is also true that he fell short. It is not that it is necessary to fall into any virtuosity but to follow a logical order to ensure what is attainable and easy first (walking well) and what is costly and arduous later (the goal and direction). There is no precise middle ground here but rather a proposal of optimums that require the ambition to do things well, in the best possible way, and to prepare for this the capacities, skills, synergies, and empathy to assume the possibility of improving the virtuous exercise of our work. It is therefore necessary to want (in the sense of desiring), to teach to want by wanting, and to learn to want by seeing how those who do it best achieve it. This, I believe, is what we could call a virtuous life.

But naturally the proposal remains in the air without a structural support. Let everyone think about his or her own apprenticeship. With all its faults and shortcomings, what would have become of us without a school to teach me what my parents and siblings did not know? If learning is shared, so is virtue. Feats, epicness, rejection, imitation, observation, and involvement are reminiscences and patterns that are given and replicated in social settings. And one thinks that it is not as difficult as some argue to find the social reason for excellence: to be better in order to make others better; to embody virtue in order to give meaning to a structure that assumes a past and to a life that moves toward a future time that continues beyond death.

Progress is adaptive, hence it is so difficult to compare across time and circumstance. Apart from the fact that the causes of delayed effects have so extended their time of repercussion, as for example atomic energy, that it becomes almost impossible to label absolute progress in certain matters except by going beyond time. Moral debates certainly have to do with human creativity to the extent that their results are concretized in lifestyles and risk and consolidate a parameter of conduct. There is an implicit discourse here on the relationship between power and freedom, that is, between the dominion of others and one's own dominion. The latter must be guaranteed at all costs for any creativity to give rise to progress.

5. Progress and Morality

WE MUST, AT THIS point, position ourselves in the interdisciplinary debate between sociology and philosophy, which separates on one side those who think that morality is of a presocial nature (a large part of traditional philosophy) and those who think that morality emanates from the social (a large part of modern sociology). The debate is relevant because the (moral) distinction between the best and the worst, between the healthy and the sick, or between the functional and the dysfunctional is a basic distinction for sociological work.

Here we do not bet on the pure constructivism of some sociologists according to which the order of relative goodness or badness of social acts and facts is under continuous construction in the minds of thinkers. But neither do we fall for the naturalism of many philosophers who claim independence between "the natural" and "the social."

The academic literature has communicated to us that there seem to be three main forms or consolidated ways of arguing moral choices: the *deontological* criterion that refers the reason of origin of moral criteria to the universalization, by whatever methods (discursive or dialogical ones are given priority) of the categorical imperative; the *culturalist* criterion that assimilates morality to cultural socialization; and the *naturalist* or neo-Aristotelian criterion that (against culturalism) defends the existence of moral absolutes as a starting point for the justification of any list of rights or prohibitions. In our opinion, none of these criteria serves as a whole on its own to morally evaluate an attitude toward the other (human or nonhuman). In this sense, we argue that starting from the certainty that there is an ultimate foundation of morality in God, there are also alternative criteria for arguing the distinction between moral and immoral social acts, so that, following the French sociologist Raymond Boudon, we argue here for a fourth approach to argue moral choices that we can call *rationalistic morality* based on the criterion of transubjectivity. We believe that this fourth approach gives us the most solid arguments for the establishment of hierarchies of values that are indispensable to bet on the capacity for improvement and progress of human beings and human societies. We do not intend to exclude anyone from the moral debate about the distinction between the best and the worst by demanding any type of sociological appropriation of morality, but we do intend that the social sciences also be considered in this debate. Our approach is different, and we hope that it can be heard on an equal basis with respect to the approaches used by other disciplines, such as philosophy or psychology, which also deal more or less centrally or incidentally with moral issues. We will gloss this point of the communitarian argumentation later on in another chapter.

Thus, the defense that communitarianism makes of moral sentiments and collective decisions through conscious processes of position-taking seems to place this school in clear opposition to the culturalism that has dominated the social sciences until very recently. Indeed, whether it be Marxism, for which morality is a conjunctural formality at the service of ulterior political ends; or Freudian psychology, which traces the roots of moral sentiments in the Oedipus complex; or behaviorism, where social conditioning indelibly marks moral convictions, the meaning of socially legitimized moral standards cannot be studied separately from the conjunctural coordinates in which social subjects move. This is also, in a certain way, what is perceived from some of Durkheim's studies, for whom it seems that social norms and the values they represent, and which are perceived as functional or positive, are so because they have been incorporated by social subjects in the process of socialization after being sifted by history.

For most of these positions, the life of social relations could not be governed from the moral point of view by anything other than the relativism that ultimately leads to the culturalist construction of moral sentiments on the assumption that there is no other basis of authority behind it. Faced with these relativistic positions, it was necessary to rescue the criteria of practical morality associated with concrete situations and circumstances in order to save an idea of society in which progress, and therefore the distinction between better and worse qualities, would be possible. At first it seemed that only two alternatives were open to save the stumbling block, represented respectively by Kantianism and Aristotelianism understood in their most comprehensive sense.

The position of Immanuel Kant (1724–1804) and his deontological argument does not seem to us to be entirely consistent for the purpose at hand since the deontological wager is, in our opinion, not very universalizable both synchronically and diachronically. Although dialogic ethics seems at first sight to have much to do with the social condition of the world, the deontological argument comes up against an obstacle that seems to us insurmountable at the theoretical level: we cannot be sure that in an interconnected society, sectorial dialogues in diverse social spaces will yield uniform results. Thus, in the caricature, if it seems right to some, it is right, and if it seems wrong to others, it is also right, so we cannot agree on which of the two positions is better, apart from which one is better taken. The deontological criterion is practical only in closed circumscriptions (the right-thinking civility of a chosen group, for example), but it does not give reasons of legitimacy to planetary solutions and, therefore, it does not have sufficient theoretical foundation to solve global problems, such as environmental problems or those that cause underdevelopment and, even more, other problems of delayed effect causes where the voices of those affected in the future must be represented without legitimacy.

Discarding Kant for the matter at hand, Aristotle appears as the clear alternative to culturalism, were it not for the fact that we have not yet brought up the social thought of Georg Wilhelm Friedrich Hegel (1770–1831). But let us take it one step at a time. Let us see what good the neo-Aristotelian position has in store for us in the face of the moral ineffectiveness of culturalist relativism.

If moral sentiments, specifically values, were the exclusive product of culture, values would be identified with counter-values and, as the American philosopher Richard Rorty (1931–2007) is not afraid to defend, virtue and vice would not differ from each other except in the eye of the beholder. From the point of view of culturalism, we cannot seriously affirm that nothing is better than its opposite; the wager for democracy as opposed to totalitarianism, for example, would only be the result of the process of socialization of democratic theory and not of its objective moral superiority, if it has one. This is why neo-Aristotelianism sees normative relativism as a social danger.

This is certainly so. Let us think of environmental problems in general, the reflection on biodiversity in particular, and of all collective actions of delayed effect, particularly the storage of toxic or radioactive waste for a long time. Where does the good begin and the convenient end? What is better, what is agreed by agreement, or what is decided as correct? Culturalism gives us criteria of convenience for some (the participants) in a framework where there may be excluded (the powerless, the future generations) and, therefore, where there is difficulty in establishing comparative criteria of improvement outside the strictly procedural ones. We may find, for example, the "excellence" of a decision to destroy the environment taken in a legitimate manner as opposed to the "perversity" of a decision to preserve the environment taken in an illegitimate manner. Logically, in the face of this nonsense, naturalism would appear as a solution to give us a judgment of excellence based on the rediscovery of human nature, so that on this basis we could operate with some objective criterion of improvement and, ultimately, of progress.

Now, the rediscovery of Aristotle solves some problems but also brings others. The communitarianism that we defend is decidedly in agreement with naturalism in that social health or excellence is susceptible to comparison in concrete and diverse social spheres and, therefore, supports the idea of moral objectivity that we can ultimately refer to God. However, the concrete way through which naturalists arrive at moral absolutes subtracts the discursive process from the social relation on the one hand, and paradoxically, on the other, in attempting to assume the role of nature, some of them break with the guarantee of the external foundation to fall into a crude idolatrous pantheism. Thus, once we find what the neo-Aristotelians call human nature, there is nothing more to talk about because either nature would not be perfectible or, for certain extremists, we should adore ourselves by worshipping it. It is true that among neo-Aristotelians today there are tendencies that point to a distinction between a hard naturalism and a soft naturalism that would be closer to rationalist positions. Delving into it is beyond our purpose here.

Some defenders of progress glimpsed this problem, and that is why at this point they went with Kant. But there, we are in the same predicament. As Vilfredo Pareto (1848–1923) argued, the deontological argument translates the "you should not steal" to "do what Mr. Kant thinks, and as he does not like you to steal, do not steal." Here, as there, we encounter a certain defenselessness. Both the categorical imperative and nature, as before culture, leave me defenseless and passive. I am led by alien intellectual avatars who have discovered for me what is good or, in the culturalist case, expedient. Is there not a way to escape this dirigisme without abandoning the objective criterion of morality? Moreover, naturalism does not explain the becoming: certain moral sentiments have changed with history, and this goes against the very idea of human nature, which is supposed to be immutable.

We think that this is the moment to save moral objectivity in our discourse by turning first to Weber and then to Hegel. Our argument, as presented by Boudon, can be summarized in the following way: neither nature nor culture, but reason. Indeed, if we take the Weberian concept of axiological rationality, we can argue that people have certain norms and values simply because they have good reasons for having them: the reasons for holding certain values are the sole cause of their distinctive enumeration and ordering. Thus, I believe that x is better than y because I have strong reasons to believe so. Moral convictions have reasons, and objectivity on the

basis of them, in the same way as any other kind of convictions. Moral objectivity is, in this sense, like any cognitive objectivity based on deliberative
reasoning on the basis of human experience: drinking fresh water instead of
salt water, not exposing oneself to parasites, helping one's neighbor, avoid-
ing corruption, acquiring a good culture, and so on.

Raymond Boudon (1934–2013) defends this position in one of the
most suggestive works to appear in the last century. The French sociologist asks himself: "We cannot imagine anyone justifying our acquiescence
to physical facts by appealing to some hidden instinct or to socialization, so
why should we invoke these mechanisms when we refer to moral normativity?" (*Le juste et le vrai. Ètudes sur lóbjectivité des valeurs et de la connaissance*, 1995, 162). If we go to life experience, we observe, on the other hand,
that there is no substantial difference between the way in which pronouncements of a positive or normative type are justified or held. In both cases,
principles and consequences are imbricated in a circular process of feedback
and revision of principles. Karl Popper (1902–1994) brilliantly defended
this argument (all knowledge, positive or normative, is provisional without ceasing to be objective), and even earlier, Georg Simmel (1858–1918)
perceived the unreason hidden behind the uncritical recognition given to
positive knowledge and the critical and suspicious doubt that threatens
normative knowledge when both types of knowledge have the same logical
legitimacy and the same circular process of continuous verification.

Notwithstanding what has been said, we still have a pending obstacle
to overcome in the defense of moral objectivity: diachrony. Here we must
call on Hegel for help. For Hegel, rationality and history are interdepen-
dently linked, and although Hegel may have been wrong about other things,
he was right about this. Thus, moral objectivity need not necessarily impose
itself on either the past or the future. The ongoing discursive process, which
is cognitive in nature, may bring about consequences and situations where
objectivity or moral truth is diverse over time, as may be the case, for example, with issues such as the taking up of arms or the death penalty itself.
Moral truths or positive truths are not historical in nature, although the
discursive process of arriving at them is always historical and continuous.

That is why moral absolutes are not immovable through time without losing, with it, their condition of absolutes within time. As can be seen,
we are not making a different discourse for moral truths than for positive
truths, which also have a historical reason of their own. In this context, we
believe that the expression "the social sense" to express moral objectivity,
thinking of the diachronic character of society, does justice to the requirements of moral truth demanded by the progressive conception (understood
as capacity for improvement) of the social order.

This discourse is novel in the panorama of sociological thought. That moral pronouncements cannot be rationally tested is an axiom on which many thinkers who disagree on almost everything else (Vilfredo Pareto, A. J. Ayer, Karl Marx, Jean-Paul Sartre, Sigmund Freud, and Émile Durkheim, for example) agree. There are, however, some who defend moral rationality outside of naturalism and whom we divide into two groups. On the one hand, there are those who rely on consequential reason: option or pronouncement x is good if its consequences are good. This group includes the functionalists, the contractualists, and the supporters of rational choice theory. On the other hand, there is, above all, Weber, who supports the axiological reason of moral criteria. His position seems to us to be the most adequate and we turn to it.

The distinction between consequential and non-consequential reasons of morality can be found in Weber's distinction between instrumental rationality and axiological rationality. The Gordian knot of the argument is the assertion that there are analytical criteria for establishing *ad casum* approximations to the moral optimum. We can arrive at this in two ways: by looking at cases where there are objectifiable evaluations that are not based on consequential criteria, and by looking at the operability of alternative criteria. We will focus on the latter point in order to try to examine whether analytical reason can indeed extrapolate and specify moral absolutes of an operative type.

We could arrive at this starting from the rationalization of the relational circumstances themselves insofar as individual subjects understand that society is made up of tacit contractual bonds whose transgression must be rejected by society itself (as is the case of the public rejection of theft). But a culturalist might argue that this is due to the very process of socialization, which in turn is indebted to the culture in which one lives. So let us go directly to feelings, so reviled by positivist sociology.

Indeed, the same feelings of justice and legitimacy that exist and are real include an affective dimension, which is rational, despite the economic neoclassicism and on which we will dwell later. The strength of the feelings of injustice is proportional to the strength of the reasons that support them. Reasons that are, by their cognitive nature, susceptible to public recognition. This is what we can call, with the previously mentioned Boudon, transubjectivity. Feelings are founded on reasons that are considered valid, in the sense that other subjects are supposed to share those same feelings on the basis of the same reasons.

Moral transubjectivity is the Weberian alternative to naturalistic objectivity, with only a few nuanced differences. We no longer speak of immutable natures or common good, but simply of moral objectivity, of moral "absolutes" (which in this discourse are not immutable, but provisional, as Popper said), and of social health or excellence. Let us say at this point that we do not intend to replace one nomenclature with another. We understand that concepts such as "common good" are more typical of philosophy, while in sociology it is more appropriate to refer to "social health." The effort we are making is to show an argument and a terminology, a properly socio-logical path, to defend the objective criteria of morality without the need to resort to the specific terminology of another knowledge.

It seems to us that in this way we save moral objectivity based on social sense and reason while at the same time clearing the way for rigid models of behavior to which neo-Aristotelian naturalism is so close. It seems to us that with this, God saved, we have given an alternative (though not opposed) foundation to that of those who defend the so-called natural morality (and law), against which we propose a rational morality of social sense. And it seems to us, finally, that we make it clear that what is best is not necessarily to be aspired to because a law says so, but simply because it is reasonable. Thus, just as there are more reasonable ways of relating to the environment than others, there are also more rational ways of relating to others than oth-ers. In other words, there are more or less reasonable cultural manifesta-tions, better or worse. Progress, then, has a place in the moral discourse.

This argumentative account is not very far from the one that could be made for those who, from economics, dedicate themselves to measure and compare progress, if it were not for the idea of progress that is present in those rooms. The controversy here lies in the dichotomy between being and having. One supposes, perhaps not quite in agreement with what is being cooked up in most faculties of economics, that what we are dealing with is to guarantee development by determining, first of all, what it is necessary to have so that, according to the circumstances of being and time that occupy us, a collective can aspire to be better and, consequently, can achieve it.

Effectively we imply here an assumption that may seem exaggerated to some, and that is that economic progress and social progress are the same thing, although it may be conceded that one becomes the other, in the un-derstanding that if it does not become neither one nor the other is really progress. In this sense, the economy is there to detect, program, and supply the necessary resources in the material order so that social progress can be materialized in immaterial countable values. We naturally speak of sustain-ability, peace, harmony, freedom, sufficiency, security, and equity, among other values that can only be measured by default and that all together make up what we have called social health (*Salud Social*, 1999).

Now, a problem arises here for the measurer that we call economist, and it is that of segmentation—an unsolvable problem if economic science were an exact science, but not if it were, which it is, a social science. And the fact is that progress lacks objectivity *a priori* but not a *sui generis* transubjectivity *a posteriori*. It is a transubjectivity segmented into life collectives that have sufficient internal reasons to legitimize a collective behavior different from that of other collectives. Here, internal discernment is important. Indeed: there are many ways to be healthy and to keep fit. There are, therefore, different progresses that we will not know for sure whether they are better or worse until history renders its judgment about the novelty, although we will have enough elements to make a judgment in the case of repetition. History also helps economy.

We advocate here a very necessary but elusive virtue in the academic sphere: humility. Progress and morality are perfectly compatible, and even more necessary, but in the case of specific collectivities we must have the benefit of the doubt in matters open to economic discernment, since in these matters it may well be necessary to assume that a given collective will have its reasons for undertaking or not undertaking a specific way of doing things. If this calls into question the validity assumed for certain development indicators in use today, specifically for the understanding of growth as an economic value, the doubt is welcome.

The arguments sketched here in defense of reason and its operability in moral issues are imbued with admiration for one of the most enlightened minds, in our opinion, of the transition from the twentieth to the twenty-first century. We refer here to Joseph Ratzinger and his defense of rational judgment. We particularly note in the text as references his Address at the University of Regensburg (September 12, 2006), the Homily in Regensburg (September 12, 2006), the Speech at Westminster Hall (September 17, 2010), and the Speech in the German Parliament (September 22, 2011).

> *The human family radicality studied by the sociology of the family, for example, brings to the fore moral presuppositions and debates of substance and topicality. The same is true of many other sociologies. Sociologists have spoken little about morality and as it is not something that escapes scientific debate, we should incorporate moral debates into our programmatic approach, dealing with the subject from our point of view and methodology with the idea of acquiring a foundation that allows us to establish our discipline with the independence required by specialized tasks and application.*

6. Moral Sociology as an Applied Sociology

WE WOULD NOT BE entirely fortunate in our discourse if we were not glimpsing the application of the knowledge we are presenting, which, in our opinion, fits in a way that many call social morality. As a small amusement and by way of a joke, we relate the witticism of a somewhat provocative professor who in a class on the social doctrine of the church said: it is neither doctrine, nor is it social, nor is it of the church.

His funny argument went like this: it is not doctrine because doctrine remains as long as it is not changed and something referring to an intrinsically changing situation cannot be understood as permanent. Labor relations are not the same as marital relations, society is not the same as the family, and industrialization and the workers' movement are not the same as sexuality. I am rather in favor, if anything, of calling it a conjunctural magisterium or magisterial thought referring to conjunctural questions. Christianity is not a sociopolitical ideology, and its doctrine is only religious and refers to permanence. It is not social, he continued, because it has not been made from the social sciences but from the misnamed human sciences and specifically from philosophy. Social philosophy is a contradiction since philosophy does not recognize society as a subject but as an aggregate. It is the missing leg of theology, and that is why I have been defending (unsuccessfully) for many years the need to be able to go to theology from sociology (which can and should be done). And it does not belong to the church, he continued, because there should not exist in the church a single thought on temporal questions. In the church there is room for both a healthy socialism that supports equality and a healthy liberalism that supports freedom. From the distinction between the temporal and the permanent comes the separation of church and state. For this reason, concluded the professor, I think that the ordinary magisterium should limit itself to illuminating realities that blur human evil *in situ et tempore*: the dignity of the human being, the irreducibility of the Sons of God, the independence of the religious sphere, justice, peace, respect, and forgiveness. It sheds light on dark (and sometimes gloomy) areas but does not give prescriptions for action. The action must be carried out in freedom by the conscience of each one without taking advantage of the church and, therefore, without calling it (its action) Christian.

The joke has a point and that is why we reproduce it. Lately, the normative character of moral obligations, which undoubtedly exists, has been emphasized to the point of blurring the actors of social action and their circumstances. A revaluation of this second aspect in the consideration makes moral inquiry much more complex but at the same time makes it more real and human. According to Etzioni, in the face of simplism and standardized case manual categories, we must rescue from oblivion the importance of normative-affective factors (NA) as opposed to the predominance of logical-empirical considerations (LE) in the cataloguing of morality arising from social action. The double thesis demonstrated in *The Moral Dimension* (1988) is that even in the aspects and situations where the LE factors seem predominant, they themselves are conditioned by NA coordinates, and that NA factors are present not only in the selection of objectives of social action but also in the choice of means. Hence the importance of grasping the moral sense as a whole and that the formation and education of the moral conscience becomes one of the central points of any educational proposal. Thus, at the basis of human education is the social.

Morality does not come only from a catalog, just as virtue is outside of one. The subjects involved, their who, also shape moral judgment. The question that usually comes up immediately in the audience when this issue is raised is whether we are then giving collective subjects the affective capacity and whether it is possible to say that human groups have feelings. Our answer is yes.

We do not propose in any way to retake outdated concepts such as the dangerous concept of "national character," but we do propose to recall that collective consciousness has its place in sociological discourse where it has been understood not in competition with individual consciousness but as a conforming and agglutinating element of social belonging. Fortunately, Durkheimians versus Freudians, moderns versus postmoderns, and communitarians versus nihilists have written and argued about this without making possible ways of understanding by introducing into the debate, as victims, freedom and the individual unconscious on the one hand, and group solidarity and identity on the other. We will not enter into this dispute, but we would like to point out the problems involved in a spatial and quantitative understanding of freedom ("my freedom goes as far as the freedom of the other begins") instead of understanding it as a qualitative challenge ("freedom goes as far as responsibility goes, beyond responsibility there is no freedom"), and a monopolistic conception of identity instead of betting on a constellation of superimposed and plural identities such as those we each have with respect to our various belongings.

In any case, it should be noted that our inclusion in communities of choice has an undeniable affective dimension regardless of its identity character or not, and that the very idea of belonging is affective because we do not live between conceptual bars that can prevent us from changing feelings and loyalties without moving from our place. Yes, in the face of legalistic positivism, we defend that the NA factors must be recognized and highlighted in the face of the push, if not imposition, of the exclusive consideration of LE factors in the elaboration of moral judgments referred and applied to social action. Both the NA and the LE make up rationality, even though certain economic theories have focused their efforts on reserving rationality exclusively for LE actions.

Morality is not only of actions but also, so to speak, of subjects. Hence, for the elaboration of moral judgments it is necessary to look not only at social acts but also at the subjects who undertake them (individuals and collectives). This calls for a totalistic vision of morality that may be complex for some but is nonetheless timely and necessary. We must understand morality, but we must also understand its subjects, and as far as we are concerned, the claim is that we must understand and know what the social consists of, a task that cannot be marginalized in any educational project or plan.

The recourse to transubjectivity that we have brought to account in the previous chapter immunizes us against the temptation to separate values and rationality. The relationship between values and affectivity seems obvious. But some still find it difficult to recognize the relationship between values and normativity. The affective component is the force of commitment to a value, so values devoid of affection are mere fictional icons that do not affect elective decisions or produce norms. He who said where there is no love there is no knowledge was not entirely wrong, since in the initial impulse to know, a certain affective interest must be manifested. Hence, normative values produce a selective exposure of information that leads to binding choices (the decision to support or reject something) even though they are reversible choices subject to rational sifting. In general, it can be said with respect to values that NA factors enhance contextualized (previously informed) choices and hinder choices deprived of LE considerations. Both affects and normative values that prescribe behaviors play positive roles and cannot be considered mere hindrances to reason in making decisions involving morality.

It is important to underline the implicit distinction we have just made between values and virtues. If values are conceptually rooted, virtues are operational. Values are ideas and objectives that can be predicated with respect to the purpose and means of situations, processes, and undertakings, while virtues are embodied in subjects of action. The difference is blurred as we sometimes use the same term to refer to a value and a virtue. We have spoken of moral, personal, social, and aesthetic values and also of human, social, cardinal, and theological virtues. Saving God, what is necessary in our opinion are two urgent priorities. The first is to maintain the distinction of opposites in both values and virtues, something that comes from the moral foundation and that qualifies as anti-values and vices, what history has sifted as such. The second is to apply the hierarchical principle to both, because otherwise and in the long run we would not be able to justify the previous priority.

This leads us, at least in passing, to speak of hierarchies, a term that raises conflicting passions in a world where equality has become an almost supreme value. We are not referring to hierarchies of subjects but only to hierarchies of values that we have established in the following order, in the form of a value pyramid with four levels that go from top to bottom, from more to less importance, and from less to more concentration and number. At the top would be the basic values, or values of being centered on those that watch over human life and its dignity; at a second level or tier would be the central values, or values of feeling centered on those that safeguard the community, health, and beliefs; in third place we would find the substantive values, or values of thinking such as democracy or tolerance; and at the base we would have the expressive values, or values of doing such as property, work, equity, or security.

Indeed, if we were to erroneously give more importance to an expressive value, such as property, as opposed to a basic value, such as freedom, which derives from the dignity of life, we would be justifying something inhuman, such as slavery. If we are all equal before the legal norm in an established system of coexistence, there are values that, regardless of personal opinions, are one above the other. And if we ask ourselves which value is above all, we must answer that this value is life, as we know human rights attests. The importance of the hierarchy of values and the primacy of life in it, however, tend to be forgotten today because for the relativism defended by the negationists, the source of value is not the objectivity of what is human but the subjectivity of autonomy.

But no, it is not autonomy that gives rise to the human but the other way around: it is the human that confers autonomy. Thus, human experimentation, the destruction of life, or torture are cases in which life is placed at the service of a superior end, of a supposedly better or more important value (the autonomy of the torturer or the pursuit of scientific discovery—health—on the part of the researcher). It is a hierarchical inversion: instead of health for life, it is life for health. Difficulties do not usually present themselves, however, in a clear way. Thus, in medicine there is an attempt to confuse with the therapeutic argument, which often puts health before life; in politics, with deterrent weapons that try to make peace compatible with the arms race; and in law, with the validity of and respect for the code that can violate justice under the pretext of compliance with the law. Whatever the wrapping, the hierarchy of values is a principle that should not be questioned on pain of protecting the rights of the established power or powers over the power of law that embodies what we understand by justice. The scale of values can be discussed and adapted to exceptional situations and circumstances, but the principle of hierarchy of values should not be violated, particularly with regard to basic values that are self-referential in terms of human dignity.

The articulation of rights and duties, of freedom and responsibility, is perhaps one of the most outstanding achievements in the process of human history. It is something that has to do with the ultimate foundation of morality, God, to whom dignity ultimately refers. It is our connection with God that makes us equally worthy to begin life's journey. Any other basis for dignity is sectarian, from citizenship of a country, to age or social background, to the claim of love by others. We are worthy because we are human creatures, because we are someone's children (*hijosdalgo*). Hence the pain produced by structural discriminations that contravene one's own or others' dignity.

Perhaps there is no harder experience in life than the injustice suffered by a power that deprives you of your dignity arbitrarily, whether it refers to your individuality or to your sociability in any of the forms in which it manifests itself. That is why today one of the greatest threats we suffer in this regard is related to the deprivation of context insofar as the rise of so-called virtual realities separates us and deprives us of the real. It is a kind of labyrinthine neo-baroque that is manifested everywhere in the drama of Sigismund in *La Vida es Sueño* (*Life is a Dream*, 1635) by Pedro Calderón.

If we go to European cultural history, we find that the period in which Renaissance and neoclassical humanism was represented plastically by vertices and straight lines is followed by another characterized by undulations and ornamental nooks and crannies that, while accentuating the peripheral, somehow hide reality. That is why the dilemma of the baroque was deception and the aspiration was disillusionment, awakening from a vital dream to recognize reality. The luck of the baroque was that behind the twists and turns of the road there was a light that contrasted precisely with the darkness and disorientation of the poses and masks (today we would say roles or profiles) of life. That light is the one that provided the faith, the truth in short, which is shown as pristine reality in contrast with the ornate ornamentation that served to enhance it and even gave it meaning. But in today's neo-baroque, is there a transcendent sense that gives reason and distinguishes what it lacks, is access to reality possible here or, on the contrary, has the line that separates the real from the virtual also become a wavy and blurred path that only disorients and loses? By looking at the past we learn from the present, and the keys of the baroque remind us that without hope there is no meaning that compensates for any difficulty. Perhaps that is why the key to our late modernity is the syndrome of loss. A labyrinth without light or exit in which the enjoyment of loss itself is proposed, turning it into a challenge of a console game of impossible survival. Certainly unworthy, we think, but is it possible to repair the injustice?

Returning to the application of values in the various areas of social entrepreneurship, a basic sociology must dare to propose lines of collective behavior and models of coexistence that give social subjects the possibility of becoming firmly embedded in the reality of a culture that does not detract from the dignity of the human. Nothing could be more opposed to this than the so-called single or correct thoughts of social legitimization that cut off and filter opinions, stories, and experiences. How have we arrived at situations where the crime of opinion is once again proposed and the dissident is penalized with academic or social exclusion? What turn have we given to our value priorities to make this possible in states that call themselves states of law? Have we confined freedom and plurality only to virtual realities that do not contest the power of any command exercising dominion in the public sphere?

The prescription we gave in *Sobrepoder* (2016) was self-mastery that also implied the renunciation of the dominion of others. We claimed there the value of restraint and the exercise of freedom. And perhaps the category of power has never been more in need of study and proposal than it is today. For a moral sociology that is also an applied sociology is undoubtedly a reflection of the first order.

> *Power struggles have made us to focus mainly on political issues forgetting the importance of the social foundations of collective life. Sociology ought to revendicate the social from the political. That poses the question to focus the academic discourse on forgotten qualities. Those that are necessary to distinguish knowledge*

*from opinion. Reason and morality are entrenched, and preserv-
ing this link may guide not only collective but also personal life.*

7. Overlapping of Moral Sociology with Other Areas of Knowledge

To THE QUESTION OF where best to place moral sociology we must answer that it is primarily and fundamentally in the field of the social sciences. However, we cannot fail to refer to certain other questions of an ontological nature that also affect several areas of knowledge.

We can say that if physics can be static or dynamic but not evolutionary, it follows that the mission of metaphysics is to discover formative processes that make each object subject to laws for its conformation as such and not as another. Similarly, if biology can be evolutionary, regressive, and adaptive but not creative, it follows that meta-biology can aspire to divine processes and states that have not yet occurred through imitation and antecedent design. Finally, if sociology has a creative dimension by establishing and coordinating human relations where and when they have not been given, it can follow that meta-sociology can aspire to invent and perfect collectivities subject to criteria of humanity. Thus, what is essential in metaphysics and probable in meta-biology is different in meta-sociology. Perhaps this is why it is often said that what is proper to the social sciences is the investigation of social change.

In any case the study of society is possible because change, like everything living in time, occurs in contexts of reality. Although social realities have proved elusive to the requirements of empirical research until relatively recently (more or less two hundred years ago, as we say) compared to other areas of knowledge, it is totally unreasonable today to enter into any scientific adventure without first having some basic knowledge of what society is, how social realities can be compared, and what implications derive from the social fact understood as a primordial fact for the science or technique in question. Next, in the mission of those who wish to enter into the study and research in question, it will be necessary, in our opinion, to show the implications that follow both for their own actions and for participation

47

in collective actions, from knowledge of the social and, fundamentally, of moral sociology.

If we refer to our epochal circumstances, the end-of-cycle crisis (or crises) of modernity calls into question one of its main foundations which, together with the activation of a planetary perspective or conscience in the face of the emergence of global challenges, calls for a substitution of the individualistic presuppositions in force today. This is what we have called on occasion the illusion of a false autonomy. For this reason, it seems to us necessary to reaffirm the constitutive human links by giving the various manifestations of the social a teaching and research attention that they have unfortunately lacked up to now. The perspective we use in this last chapter of this part is, as we have also done before, the communitarian one.

Human communities are not conventional, they are not the result of a convenient choice on the part of autonomous adults. It is rather the other way around, since our identities of space and origin are not the result of choice, even if there is the possibility of choosing various other "we" of a vocational, occupational, neighborhood, or recreational nature. In the I-we relationship there is a permanent search for balance that must converge in mutual receptive understanding. Thus, the expression used by Etzioni of receptive communities tries to grant an appropriate status with relational meaning both to the individual and to the various communities that ultimately make him/her concrete. Individual and community make and need each other to the point that it should be noted that the self needs some of us in order to be who it is. From the family, the language, the belief, the time and place, or the citizenship card, to the friendships, educational institutions, tastes, and hobbies without which it (without those we) would not be who it is.

There are two concepts in relation to the subject that we would like to gloss on as I understand that they shed light on what it means to understand and properly value our communal character, threatened both by individualism on the one hand and egalitarianism on the other, and that could well help other areas of knowledge to understand the social. I am referring to fragmentation and strangeness.

The consciousness of the "we" is not a mere feeling. This has always been difficult to accept for liberalism, which has celebrated autonomy as the negation of mutual dependencies. This has resulted in the emergence of social disintegration and the consequent phenomenon of fragmentation. Fragmentation, however, constitutes a serious obstacle to understanding society as a continuous whole. This is not a theoretical obstacle but an eminently practical one, and it denounces the growing difficulty caused by individualism to see society as something different and prior to the aggregation of individuals. We understand that the fragmentation we are suffering from has occurred at four main levels.

Productive fragmentation is a consequence of the process of specialization that culminates in the new division of labor that ends up introducing, in a more and more accentuated way, the implementation of new technologies in a labor fabric that has mostly lost its cooperative sense. Productive fragmentation is not the simple division of tasks and the organization of work in a chain that F. W. Taylor and Henri Fayol studied in their day and that Henry Ford implemented (Fordism). We are referring to the effective disengagement of the participants in the production process that goes hand in hand with phenomena such as corporate delocalization and globalization. The praxis of the continuous system of production has been lost, which makes the idea of envisioning a complete process of transformation of goods tremendously complex, and without this idea it is practically impossible to delimit collective responsibilities for the whole of this process. With super-specialization, it is very difficult to cement bonds of co-responsibility and belonging among all those involved in the same product.

On the other hand, *social fragmentation* is a consequence of the increase in inequality that has occurred in recent years. This phenomenon is difficult to explain for neoclassical economists, but the fact is obvious: in recent years, the gap in income distribution between the North and the South has increased, at the same time as it has also increased in paradigmatic countries such as the USA, where the gap between the richest 20 percent of the population and the poorest 20 percent of the population has widened. The causes do not derive solely from the malfunctioning of economic policies. One aspect to consider is that income inequalities could also point to cultural inequalities that are in themselves positive. Indeed, measuring wealth in terms of percentage increases in GDP, which is how it is measured, is tremendously narrow. A narrowness that manifests itself in not giving value to infrastructures and in ignoring non-monetizable wealth, such as moral wealth and what this entails, such as indicators of family stability and solidarity, among others, which reveal symptoms of health and social wellbeing. In the assumption of satisfaction of basic needs, different levels of wealth could well represent the difference between those who quantify everything in monetary terms and those who have other objectives in life. In any case, in our opinion, social fragmentation is rooted in the lack of the concept of sufficiency in the current economic culture.

Structural fragmentation represents the breaking of the world into a thousand pieces; that is, the multiplication of conflicts resulting from the search for recognition and the increase in the levels of action of more subjects who interact more, which produces an increase in social complexity.

The multiplication of power generated by new spheres of innovation has been countered by the parallel impulse of demands for autonomy. The result is that the post-, hyper-, or late-modern aspiration (let's not get into the terminology) has replaced the yearning for freedom that the twentieth century began with the desire for independence with which the twenty-first century is beginning. We want to be more and more independent and autonomous because we feel more and more constrained. We have neither mastered our tools (our means) nor our aspirations (our ends) and consequently we feel bewildered. The dizzying pace of events threatens our forecasts; therefore, the abandonment of the desire to control everything produces ambivalence: a feeling of riding a runaway horse where the important thing is to stay on top of it and not where to go. In the end, the multiplication of the demands to which we are subjected, which is what structural fragmentation ultimately boils down to, makes us discover that we consume complexity, and this produces the illusion of satisfying our aspiration for autonomy and independence.

There is another context in which fragmentation must be analyzed more calmly. It is a matter of examining what the consolidation of the spirit of the Enlightenment meant in the development of what we call modernity: the emergence of the self as the primordial social subject. In the analysis of the cultural changes produced by the culture of modernity, perhaps the most interesting is that of the loss of a sense of community and the parallel rise of individualism. Individualism produces a multiplication of subjects of consumption (atomization) without having to diversify the social offer. This individualism leads to a *cultural fragmentation*. The first cause of this fourth fragmentation has been the attempt to replace the community as a social category in the face of the rise of individualism.

If we recall, the study of the communitarian or associative character of modern societies belongs to the very origin of sociology. The Durkheimian distinction between organic and mechanical solidarity is like the distinction enshrined by Ferdinand Tönnies (1855–1936) between community and association. The community dimension creates identity and gives precedence to the social, while the associative dimension gives precedence to the individual without creating identity. Tönnies's argument was that, although both coexist, the so-called modernization process that follows industrialization produces an increase in the type of associative relations to the detriment of community relations. Weber, in point 9 of the first chapter of his seminal *Economy and Society*, also used the distinction. However, he further blurs the contours of conceptual separation by affirming that every social relation, even that most strictly originated in the pursuit of its own individual end, can give rise to social values. In any case, the passage from the predominance of the community to that of association is universally detectable in the so-called developed countries where the turn toward association to the detriment of the community culminates in individualism, which is immediately confirmed culturally as the result of a genuinely modern vision.

Individualism, as a cultural, epiphenomenal manifestation of late modernity, marks the decline of the social spirit that gave birth to modern culture itself. This is recognized even by the very apologists of modernity (Zygmunt Bauman, Anthony Giddens), although they maintain that modernity itself contains the seeds for overcoming its decadence. We allow ourselves to doubt the diagnosis. Fragmentation is one of the signs of the moral decadence of the present time because it prevents us from seeing the whole and all. On the other hand, fragmentation annuls responsibility and minimizes us as individual subjects, not incorporating the annulled responsibilities to any recognizable collective subject. A kind of "nobody is responsible here" that turns us all into obedient memos of obtuse inertias that try to content us with the trifle of a salary, a minimum income, or a security encapsulated in quasi-slavery. Fragmentation thus understood can then be interpreted as a structure of evil, however much other disciplines may defend it with criteria of efficiency and competitiveness.

Let us move on to the other concept—that of strangeness. There is much talk of integration and welcoming, and it is good that this is the case because its absence denotes a decline in solidarity and a loss of collective health in our societies. This, however, should not make us forget an essential aspect of the life of our communities, which is the knowledge of their limits. Communities exist because they differentiate and therefore exclude. Exclusion—i.e., the recognition that there is space and life beyond the community—is a foundation of its very existence. We call this phenomenon strangeness.

Strangeness is a consequence of distinction—that is, of plurality. Communities have boundaries and gates based ultimately on the differentiation of opposites. That is why strangeness is a necessity that is no longer explanatory but constitutive of communities. It seems paradoxical, but here, as in so many aspects of life, exclusion is what justifies inclusion. The first anthropologists clumsily intuited this truth when they tried to explain the origin of the family in the prohibition of incest (an inclusive trait). Without estrangement, without the distinction between us and you, there is no possibility of self-knowledge once we have understood that humans are relational beings. Without strangeness and the consequent capacity to distinguish ourselves, the understanding of our identity would escape us, especially if we take into account that the most identitarian communities, such as language, religion, and above all the family, are not generally communities of choice.

This is of radical importance for understanding ourselves as human beings and is a necessary objectification for the understanding of the social. Something similar happens with other distinctions of principle. Thus, without the distinction between the optimum and the appalling, or between the best and the worst, it is impossible to differentiate progress from decadence, and without this distinction neither economics nor sociology is possible. On the other hand, the distinction between health and disease makes possible the practice of medicine, and the distinction between the praiseworthy and the punishable makes possible the practice of law.

Seeing the recognition and the need to safeguard the differences between the various *us* and *you* it is necessary to be able to understand ourselves as equally free. Some think that the recognition of strangeness is the same as defending the inequality of human beings and that it is not strangeness that we must defend but equality that must converge in a context of maximum inclusion. This position implies, as can be understood, the express prohibition of the existence of communities, which in turn is, in our opinion, an attack on freedom. Strangeness implies distinction but not incommunicability. Strangeness should not be understood as an insurmountable line but as a demarcation. From the point of view of political realities, the understanding of strangeness as a necessary limit of the community leads to healthy conclusions that we can explain axiomatically as follows: maximum diversity from the inside, maximum unity from the outside.

The maximum unity from the outside is the strangeness that occurs in differentiated units that perceive each other as all different, all of them even of the same kind. Thus, several states, several teams, several identity loyalties. The internal unity of each of the "alls" makes them mutually exclusive units; therefore, they can be counted. The maximum diversity behind closed doors points to the multiplicity of communities recognized as such that can also be superimposed in such a way that the multiple *us* that are in each one can hardly be found in another individual. This plurality of communitarian ascription is in our opinion the most solid foundation for individuation: my "wes" makes me different. It is therefore understandable that communitarians refer to communities in the plural.

The ultimate reason for the differentiation between communities, that is, for the strangeness that marks the limits of the collective, is its survival to increase the freedom of the human being. In this sense we think that the raison d'être of the state is also freedom: to promote, increase, and defend it. There are those who think that the raison d'être of the state is equality, and it is not strange that these same people think that communities are an obstacle to equality. Even if they are wrong about what constitutes the mission of the state, they are not wrong that communities are an obstacle to equality as they understand it. For communitarianism, equality is to be constructed not by trying to replace or suppress the exclusion to which strangeness gives rise but precisely by accepting it: we are all equal on the basis that we are equally strangers. We have constitutive community boundaries (we are all equally familiar, even from different families; equally citizens, even from different countries; equally subject to human rights and duties), and we also have deliberative community boundaries that we have granted ourselves on the basis of our choices—choices that anyone else could have made as well.

As far as freedom is concerned, the state, like other communities, justifies itself as its guarantor. And it is precisely in the execution of this guarantee that the deliberative freedom of any subject must be prevented from being infringed by means of prior distributions. Thus, redistributive policies or sectoral incentives are aimed at promoting freedom, and in this sense, it can be understood that equality policies are aimed at freedom, never the other way around. Equality cannot be considered the goal of government action because this necessarily leads to the infringement of liberties and the proscription of communities.

Many of those who place liberty as a function of equality and not the other way around, accepting as a factual impossibility the suppression of communities in practice, advocate tolerating them, but only insofar as they are confined to what they call the private sphere. For them, the public sphere must be reserved for an exclusive and monopolistic power: the power of the state. In addition to the totalitarian shadow that can be guessed behind this position, it is necessary to criticize here an anthropological error of base because the human being deprived of his communities, of the constitutive and deliberative benevolent communities that shape him as what he is, ceases to be human. No wonder we think that the eagerness to ignore the community is an anti-humanism at the speculative level and a tyranny at the political level.

It is also a fictional aspiration that is out of touch with reality, for we can only imagine the reconfiguration of the totalitarian state in apocalyptic dystopias. Strangeness concretizes our responsibility in the proximate, which is the real par excellence. It is the very and precise concretion of responsibility. Subjects who fail to assume their responsibilities can hardly be recognized as such (responsible) by advocating how other subjects should face theirs. Reality is a continuum, and without realism there is no possibility of making a social inquiry that deserves the label of scientific. It is first necessary to situate oneself so that the journey, even if it is only a comprehensive one, can be successful. Any who refers to several *us* that must be recognized.

As we can see, there is bread for everyone. The implications of moral sociology led us to various sociologies crossing the area to other disciplines with fortunate narratives on freedom and liberties, political order, production and consumption systems, or the educational system itself. The stories involved may be told in one way or another, but this is already part of the expertise, and it would be good if other experts in other fields were also involved in the task of making visible in their area the implications of moral sociology for their specific field.

> Much has been spoken of culture wars nowadays. Many understand it wrongly as if the field of battle were outside our own self. To clear up the sky to realize who we are in our distinctive and unique tangle of communal relationships impels us to make moral commitments and decisions. And the more we know about the scope, hierarchy, and importance of our belongings, the better it will be not only for perfecting ourselves but also for the proposals we offer or receive from others to improve our shared existence.

PART 2

FOR ANY ACADEMIC TO write without quotations or footnotes, besides being a liberation, is a sign of trust with the reader that can only be assumed if the author has already entered the venerable age, which is my case. Thank you for allowing me to do so. In this part 2, I write, and I have not always done so, without self-censorship or vain prurience. This is a popular essay for a university audience. I say what I think freely and without the need to subject myself to the rigors of a scholarly text. Evidently, on the other hand, I pour here my readings and reflections of many years on topics that I believe are important, not only to me but also to those who are concerned about the future of the world.

We are in the age of concern. Not of a concern born of suspicion but of distrust. We are no longer concerned about the strength of the hypothetical adversary but about the constancy of our own weakness. A moral weakness, more than an instrumental weakness, of which we have palpable evidence in the history of the traumatic twentieth century, which we are beginning to see with perspective and whose legacies and experiences in the twenty-first century frighten us.

The result is a synthetic essay of leisurely reading, and I hope that, in the opinion of those who read it, it will also be engrossing. Apart from the fact that in books of this style the pages begin to frighten, at this age one can only write concisely, in the hope that, God willing, one will have the opportunity to go into the subject in greater depth if another does not do so first. In any case, it has come out complete, and it is what I wanted to say. The forms have been the result of a conscious choice. As I say, I write for a reading and concerned public, but without disciplinary labels or positional conditioning. Thus, I hope that this book will be useful to my students and disciples as well as to the general reader interested in the topics I deal with.

One can say that here I write about what I think I know. I have devoted myself to the profession of sociology for many years and have worked through all these issues in my work, but I am not writing now exclusively for my colleagues. Nor am I writing so that no one will listen to me. I write in case someone understands what I mean and why I say it, even without necessarily sharing anything I say. It is an old professor's view of the time to come, given his experience with the time that has already come.

And we begin this second part with two issues that are, in my opinion, the conditioning foundation of a possible future: reality and practical morality. Among other reasons, because one of the root causes of the fact that the world we know is tottering and showing the cracks that denote its already scarce viability is precisely the flight from reality and the associated loss of moral strength. And without these foundations there is no building that can stand.

1. Reality

THERE IS NO DOUBT that it is convenient to have an impact on the realities that make up existence since the difficulty of situating oneself in it is becoming more and more evident. Perhaps one of the important difficulties of our time in doing science, and implicitly I make the necessary distinction between science and opinion, is that of recognizing reality. We are, as subjects who are part of it, intimidated. As it were, we contemplate many and varied realities to the extent that never in history have we been subjected to more powers, and each power tries to involve us in its reality by inserting us, sometimes forcefully, within it.

I am not referring only to political powers, even if they are the most obvious, but above all to media powers that have never been so important. They affect our lives, particularly our relational lives, to an extent that could hardly have been imagined not so long ago. We have never been more obliged to accept and commune with alternative realities, and this puts us in the position of recognition: how do I distinguish what is real from what is not real, what is real from what is invented or virtual, and, consequently, where do I stand before those questions, so often asked of philosophy, of who I am and where I am? These questions are of pressing topicality, not only in general but particularly for specific sectors of the population, such as young people.

I have sometimes said that my experience as a teacher has been, from a certain point of view, disappointing. I have never been able to realize myself in the contemplation of improvements in the task of educating the coming generations. I have gone through or, it would be better to say, I have suffered many education plans and laws, each one worse and worse. Nevertheless, the training with which students enter university each year is more deficient, to levels that would astonish a neophyte. The ability to defend one's own criteria, if one has any, is increasingly scarce, and the level with which students leave university is recurrently inferior to that of the previous year.

There is no doubt that the university is in decline, and I think that one of the reasons for this decline is precisely the prevailing discourse on reality. Without recognizing it, one cannot understand what and why what is ending is ending, nor what may be what is to come.

I am going to jot down some reflections in this regard that I hope will help, if not to understand, and here I am a bit selfish, to understand myself. To understand myself and at the same time to help the reader to understand him/herself too, because reality, to use a fortunate saying, is not what it used to be. Yes, to begin with, reality is now much more complex and difficult to recognize.

The complexity comes, in part, from us, who have distanced ourselves from it, and this remoteness does not allow us to accept it with precision. For the purposes of a gradual approximation, I dare to distinguish three types of realities that make up a whole. On the one hand, there is what we could call *socionatural reality*. Here we have not only the reality previously conceived as mere nature but also the artificial reality that is physical or material reality; the symbolic reality that shapes and builds culture; and the relational realities that shape human interaction and dependence. All this makes up a reality that I call socionatural to emphasize that, today, we cannot distinguish society from nature as blithely as before. Nature is already society; we have included it, we have subdued it, we can destroy it, and we can destroy ourselves by destroying our vital sustenance.

The affirmation of the social condition of nature has not been glossed over until very recently. It is that famous treasure trove of which I have once written. There is what is created directly by God, and what is created indirectly by God through us, through our reason or unreason. There is the natural and the artificial, the physical, the symbolic, and the social. One might say: well, you have already said it, all that is reality. Well, not quite. In addition to this reality, which we could say is a reality built and recognizable to us, in the broadest possible sense, there are two other realities that we must take into consideration.

On the one hand, we point out a second reality that we can call *supernatural*. We have called the previous one socionatural, and we can call this one supernatural or spiritual. It transcends us. It is a reality created to the extent that in the face of the divine reality, feeling challenged, we orient ourselves and change in this regard. This assumes that God exists, a premise from which I start. They are surprised by this and say: hey, you will have to demonstrate this. Although later we will dwell on it, I do not have to prove it in the same way that I do not have to prove that other observable things exist even if one has not seen them directly or indirectly (which is not my case in the subject in question). There are witnesses, and that should be enough. We cannot demand of supernatural reality criteria of verification different from those we demand for other realities. In the purely supernatural spiritual there is God, there are those who are with God and there we will be, God willing. Many, many people organize their lives and their actions in this world in the face of this reality; therefore, this reality is not only a supernatural reality but also a reality for us, let us say it: in a way, it is also earthly. A reality to which we should refer, otherwise we would be missing something important, which at the same time would affect our very location and self-understanding.

On the other hand, we have a third reality, which is that arcane and *self-referential reality* of our desires, ideals, thoughts, judgments, emotions, and feelings, which remain only within us but which exist. It is the I think this, I have imagined such a thing, I have really imagined it, it exists only in me, but it exists, and I cannot deny its condition because I would be denying myself.

These three realities are, in my opinion, the three legs of the table on which existence rests. We can call these three supports, we, God, and I: the socionatural reality, the supernatural reality, and the consciousness or thought reality. But these three realities support and sustain an existence that is not only made up of presences. Existence is also made up of absences that have been and absences that are not yet, insofar as existence is life and time. Rather, life that passes through time and not so much time that passes through life.

We must not confuse the terms. I do not think it is necessary to explain here, it is beyond our purpose, the difference between truth, realities, and existences, when we refer to logical and provisional certainties (there is truth), when we refer to conformations that affect our insertion in life (there are the relational realities and as far as past lives are concerned there are the absences), or when we discover the radicality of the present (there is the shared existence that refers to this triple reality). Reality thus understood situates us in life, we must say, with a certain humility. The humility of thinking of ourselves as made to measure for reality (for it) and not the other way around.

The challenge is to realize it. To keep our feet on the ground. Reality is here, and whether we want it or not, we are part of it. It is impossible to avoid it, so what is wrong with us, that we don't like it, let's improve it by improving ourselves. The old materialism does not give much more of itself, and we must open ourselves to the complexity of an existence and a reality more in tune with the mystery of our life.

For those of us who studied in those old curricula, all this reminds us of that old reflection on the states of matter. I studied in my younger years that matter can be living or inert, and I mistakenly inferred that inert matter was dead matter. Today we know that everything is alive because the atoms are not inert, and inside, the subatomic particles rotate; there are movements that we have not yet studied and that pose us decisive questions. Is there anything that is "materially" dead? What does the soul have to do with all this? These are recurring questions to be asked to distinguish matter from spirit and to see if there is something that is purely and truly nonmaterial, that does not have a material consequence. Or, similarly, if there is something that is not supernatural even if it does not have a material consequence. These are very difficult distinctions to make that have brought cosmological knowledge (or lack of knowledge) to the fore.

May the reader forgive me for daring thus, at this moment, to navigate in the tempestuous sea of abstraction, but the questioning is necessary, if only to realize how ill-equipped we are to face the drastic changes in which we are immersed. We will lower the navigation level later. To recognize reality, to situate it and to situate ourselves, is necessary to decipher our waning in the face of the changes that, inevitably, we should consider for survival beyond our life span. And to this writer, cosmology, nowadays so far removed from curricula (although not so far from cinematographic fiction) seems more than important.

Thus, in the specialized literature, as we said, we no longer speak so much of biospheric realities as of noospheric realities, which point to an integration and relationship between reason and reality, parallel to that between nature and society. But we could go even further, noting that these premises belong to a universalist framework in which we can recognize ourselves. Indeed, we do not know if other universes exist, but there is no reason to avoid pointing to this possibility, which we could call pluriversality. What if our universe did not constitute the frontiers of a reality but was part of other realities? Is the void empty, is there nothing there? These are questions that have consumed many neurons of philosophers and cosmologists now and in past times, and I believe that, just stating them, they serve our purpose, which is to glimpse the complexity of the concept of reality as well as to humble us and show us how much we still must know.

I have consciously posed all these questions in the opening chapter of this second part, which paradoxically we refer to as *praxis*. Here, we can say, there is a trick, because one believes that the best way to become clear with reality is not to become clear at all. To perceive its complexity and to lose oneself in it, to always look for oneself, because we will always be lost. Existence is incomprehensible and surpasses us all, as in the redundant saying. If the socionatural reality already seems to us, as we have proposed it, so global, so great, so incomprehensible, what to do when we add to it the supernatural reality and the arcane of the inner self? How to orient ourselves is difficult, certainly, but we live in that difficulty and to orient ourselves in life is, first, to perceive the difficulty of the undertaking. Only when we accept the legitimacy and opportunity of the questions, at that moment, we will be equipped with the necessary tools to be able to overcome the doubts and propose correct solutions. These tools have a lot to do with culture, a lot to do with study, and very little to do, in my opinion, with screens. I am sorry, but I am one of those who think that the so-called virtual reality is something else, as I will explain, if I may, below.

2. Unreality

UNREALISM IS A PRODUCT of relativistic subjectivism. The unbridled speculation that promotes subjectivity without barriers needs to rely more on the
empirical and the implicit certainty of the data. Hence the importance of
advocating more sociology and more quantitative methodology (less ideology) in curricula, so as not to be always in the clouds. Perhaps this is too
much to ask, but let's take it one step at a time.

Unreality is too present in our lives, to the point that I think it has
somehow turned existence upside down. And the fact is that the balanced
relationship between the realms of reality has been disrupted lately. The
domains, the realms of reality, we have said that there are three: the socionatural reality, the supernatural reality, and the inner reality or internal
forum, and there is a relationship between these three realities that is necessary to maintain the consciousness of existence without adding conceptual
obstacles to an already complex task. This relationship, however, has been
disrupted lately by the exaggerated growth of the so-called "subjective reality" (some call it hyperreality, but I don't like the term). This exaggeration
has moved existence to a point of imbalance. It has gone from bare realism
and from accepting that binomial dichotomy between realism and idealism, to talk about adjectival realism, among which there is something very
funny for someone who is not dedicated to speculation: something they call
critical realism.

One does not quite understand what this critical realism is, unless it
refers to a rejection of reality that motivates an attempt to replace it with
other parallel realities, imagined or speculated. What seems clear to me is
that the predominance in current thought of this critical realism has become
a preponderance, also, of relativistic subjectivism and, I fear, as has almost
always happened, that from relativistic subjectivism or from relativism in
general there is now the need to resort again to some form of absolutism.

It is the danger of the rejection of reality that entails that this third realm of realism, the internal realm, becomes or aspires to become the dominator of the other two realms, the socionatural reality and the supernatural reality. Realism, in my modest opinion, should not be overly adjectivized, which is why I do not like the expression "to situate oneself in reality." Rather, I think we should "recognize ourselves in reality," because "situating ourselves in reality" can lead us to think that it is reality that has to be situated, or rather, that we are the ones who have to situate reality.

I was amused by an advertising campaign I saw on the net that encourages everyone to define their own reality. Redefine reality, but how can anyone dare to do so? Some are already openly stating that the dominant reality is the subjective reality, and that this subjective reality is the one that necessarily conditions the other two realities, the socionatural and the spiritual. Well, let's stop the cart. There is a misconception here. We sociologists have always tried to introduce some quantitative criteria in the measurement of reality. Above all, socionatural reality is susceptible to measurement while those other pseudo-realities or unrealities, in which subjectivism and relativism predominate, are very difficult to measure. They do not admit the accounting criterion. Reality has aspects that are unmeasurable and uncountable, but it also has others that necessarily are, and to leave or disregard those aspects, more or less empirical, is also to leave reality (a possible euphemism).

We were saying that of recognizing ourselves and not situating it as we please. Reality situates us in existence, not the other way around, despite this network advertising campaign. The consequences of unrealism are serious. It prevents us from being constant because we admit from the outset the changing nature of reality to the observer's liking. The unrealists do us no favors when they say that all reality is the result of a social construction. No, contrary to popular belief, sociologists do not say that. Social construction may be present and indeed is present in some aspects of socionatural reality, in none of those of supernatural reality, and in some aspects of subjective reality, but only in some, not in all. Reality admits, and there is part of it, that it is a social construct, of which there is no doubt, but not all reality is a social construct. Therefore, when from unrealism we preach with too much faith in creative subjectivism, then we fall into very lacerating scourges: the absence of constancy and commitment are two of them, because as reality changes or I can redefine reality, then if I committed myself to another reality, I have no duty or responsibility toward it because now I am in another one. The concept of the world disappears, it does not exist, because nothing is permanent and neither am I: I have no obligation to be constant, since I can produce successive and infinite realities (and if you do not trust your reality, how can I trust and rely on you, one might add).

There has been much criticism of the "intrusion" of psychology into sociology, and I bring it up here because certain aspects of unrealism have to do with that psychologistic exaggeration or intrusion. In the end, the problem becomes the lack of self-recognition, a knowing oneself to be limited by a reality, which implies a humility that we cannot deny. Thus, this exacerbation of desire and identity ambition, which is observed everywhere, has at its origin a syndrome of loss. I do not know where I am, I do not know who I am, because I have displaced reality; in the end, I have placed myself in unreality. It is a sometimes uncontrollable confusion that prevents us from recognizing fiction where it is.

We should not reject all fiction. Fiction has a positive function, but to confuse fiction with reality is, after all, to confuse oneself. Not to distinguish, as when they used to say "he is on the moon": in his undistinguished world. Not to distinguish that moon and that world from what really surrounds us, not referring exclusively to the material but also to the cultural, is an attempt at imposition as well. Relativism, although it preaches that all subjectivities have value, in the end, ends up trying to impose some subjectivities on others. For example, when it rules on collective memories, so fashionable.

Going away from reality by affirming oneself in unrealism brings pernicious social consequences, apart from the fact that there are painful and even pathological consequences for the individual himself. Some of them are funny, like that story about the medieval monk who studied the sea without ever having seen it. When he saw it for the first time in his life, in his old age, he said to himself that this sea is of no use to me, as if to say: my reality was better than this one here.

Unrealism leads us to ontological negationism. Everything that is not me is a hallucination that is, in the end, the fruit of addiction to virtual realities. That is why there are so many pathological addictions nowadays. That is why screens dominate us, they project unreality or subjective realities that should not have come from the person who thought them up. Unrealism molds us culturally. The dictatorship, the tyranny of single thought, is one of the connotations of unrealism. It is necessary, we repeat, to recognize ourselves, not to situate ourselves, and reality situates us. It is preexistent to ourselves. Here is that radicality that we have always defended and that we will never tire of repeating: we are fundamentally children, we are born into a society that already exists.

Reality is unitary and unrealism isolates us from ourselves. From my reason to your reason, from my truths to yours, and from my reality to yours; from my reasons of yesterday to my reasons of today, or from my reality of yesterday to my reality of today, there is, in all this, a short step. Embracing unrealism, considering impossible the pretension of understanding and recognizing a unitary reality, implies denying the possibility of communicating with each other. We end up speaking different languages to the point that, in the end, we may think that the only thing words are good for is to communicate with oneself and, if anything, with those who share the same reality as me: my virtual tribe.

The enthronement of the digital algorithm is not alien to this dehumanizing pretension of unrealism. Some people confuse the algorithm with the data, but they are really opposites. One is pretentious and the other factual; one can be plausible (some confuse plausibility with truth) while the other is true; one looks to a future under construction and the other to a concluded and irrefutable event. Algorithmic proliferation and the digitization of existence, in fact, crumple the data and lock it up under seven keys. Data uncovers reality, and this is of less interest than the possibility of constructing it (or is it replacing it?) provided by the algorithm.

Society is not a consequence of our design; on the contrary, if anything, we are a consequence of the social design. There is something precedent, not chosen, or eligible by us: our parents, our time, our language, and our place. How curious that now all these kinds of linguistic corrections about gender are being promulgated, as if assuming that everything is a construct in which the results must be continually corrected. No, no, stop, we cannot get out of time, we cannot get out of things that constitute us: those parts of reality that do not radically depend on us. No: let us open our reason and realize we are not the center, we are not gods.

There are recurring sayings in the academy as the answer to the question, "What is the great evil of academics?" As it goes, the answer points to vanity, and vanity has a lot to do with pride: it centers everything on oneself. In the end, unrealism centers everything in oneself. One is amazed by the little critical capacity that often appears in the academy, how there are mediocre authors who repeat what praises the media powers and who are elevated as gurus of culture, while there are others who try to cancel simply for being part of the dissent and criticism. The culture of cancellation, or rather, the unculture of cancellation, is, in the end, the denial of reality elevated to a political category. To deny reality and to aim at unrealism is, in short, to deny ourselves: to erase ourselves from rational life.

Denialism shoots through the bull's eye, and from denying others it quickly passes to self-denial. It is not surprising, therefore, that suicide and euthanasia are on the rise. The loss of ontological referents ends up advocating euthanasia (we will return to this later). At the genesis of the defense of individual euthanasia is that my life becomes the fruit of my design and, subsequently, that the others are also the fruit of theirs, with the result that unreality renders life incomprehensible. That is why one of the recipes I usually point out to recognize ourselves collectively inserted in a preexisting reality is to advocate for data. Especially in the academy, where the appropriate methodology is supposed to be available. With this I defend and call for a little more sociology, a little more measurement, and a little less speculation. We must save the empirical; we ought to save that intimate and balanced relationship of those realities that make up existence—the socionatural, the supernatural, and the inner individual. So, more sociology, please.

Having established this, which was a solid and necessary starting premise for what follows, we conclude this dissertation on reality that we made in the previous chapter and on unreality in this one, with a consideration of principles. Any human future, considering what has come, must be based on a shared morality that makes existence a sustainable life. It is not a requirement that can be postponed, avoidable or dispensable, as it may have been in other past times. Our future, beyond our life span, will be moral or it will not be.

3. Practical Morality

As we stated in the first part, sociology is indispensable to argue morality in the present time. The social subject, which must be recognized as such, is a moral subject, and his social acts are susceptible to moral judgment. In this task of rescuing a morality for survival, ecology and economics will be of great use to us. We maintain the level of abstraction of the last two chapters, but we promise that in the fourth chapter of this part we will go down to earth. Underlining what we said earlier, the outline we will follow in this chapter goes through: the foundations of moral sociology and acts and the social subject; some matters related to virtues and structures of virtue; and a review of transsubjectivity.

Sociologists, surprising though it may be to some, have something to say about moral acts, and it is rather a lot than a little. I am referring not only to what they call social ethics but also to the foundations of morality. Classical morality has studied, or has pretended to study with a propositional character, a field of action focused on the question of human acts. But visualizing them from a mainly speculative viewpoint, it has referred to human acts in general and, more specifically, to the human act of the individual, what certain philosophy calls person, and not so much to the human acts of the collective, of the group. The writer here defends that social acts are human acts and vice versa, and this gives us reason to speak, as we have seen in the first part, of moral sociology as a perspective that cannot be assimilated to classical morality.

Thus, the end of morality, both for moralists and sociologists, may be the same: happiness and benevolence that procures the good. The external spectator may also be the same, God, although for certain modern, classical advocates of modernity, morality should set God aside and put the (dialogical) agreement instead. Let us point out that the difference between one and the other, moral sociology and the so-called classical morality that studies mainly philosophy, is the subject. The subject is different: we sociologists, when speaking of the moral subject, do not look so much at the individual person as at the human group and, more specifically, at a human group that we have labeled us-all-always.

It is about *us*, humans; *all* is the spatial whole, insofar as never before as now have we been aware of living in a culture and society that we call global; and *always* is the diachrony, and there we incorporate the (moral) rights of those who have preceded us and those who will replace us. This appreciation of the moral subject that we call us—all of us—is always present and necessary when studying the environment from a point of view that we have dared to call eco-rationalism, and there we can distinguish between positive social acts and negative social acts. The social act properly understood, in a positive sense, is always an act of service that implies binding relationships between those people who make up the subject that we have baptized as we-all-always. On the contrary, the negative social act is a victimizing act that produces damage—in the family, in society in general, in the environment, or in other realms.

What we draw from this is that when we speak of a social act performed by a collective subject, we are also giving rise to the protagonism of a social conscience, of a collective conscience, which, unlike how one of the first sociologists, Émile Durkheim, explained it, we understand as a collective conscience that is born from sharing responsibilities and not so much from sharing beliefs.

The importance of the social act for the study of morality is, in our opinion, fundamental. It is more or less clear when studying the environment and social acts within the framework of a general good (we will return to this later). But it is also relevant when studying the economy, especially from a socioeconomic perspective. In this regard, we refer to Amitai Etzioni, who says that moral factors and social acts are necessarily intertwined. This is true not only when it comes to aiming at ends but also when it comes to the use of means.

Morality is not only of actions but also of subjects, and both when speaking in economics and from the point of view of ecology, these subjects are social subjects. If we go to the social act and look for the protagonist, we should speak of that we-all-always that has remained hidden to individualism. The preponderance of neoclassical economics, of neoliberalism as it is called, has not allowed us to see this social subject clearly, has not even allowed us to catalog it, and, consequently, has prevented us from giving it responsibility. Nevertheless, it is necessary to give it to him since he is a moral subject of whom a moral judgment can be made.

From the point of view of individualism, this is an aberration. It is an aberration denounced by the very title of a book by Etzioni, *My Brother's*

Keeper. The individualist says no, that we should not give him moral owner-ship or demand responsibility, but the sociologist is obliged to say yes, we are the guardians, we are responsible for our brothers, and this responsibil-ity is concretized, among other ways, in the social action of the collective subject, of the human group, and, of course, in the conceptualization and acceptance of the social conscience.

There are many people who are afraid of the terminology of social conscience as if that social conscience could supplant individual conscience, which it does not supplant, or as if that social conscience could undermine freedom, which it does not undermine. It is true that it is necessary to un-derstand social conscience correctly. It may be, and I recognize that perhaps some followers of Durkheim have taken this social conscience too far to the point of putting individual freedom in quotation marks, but when we look at responsibility, then we understand that this social conscience makes sense. In this respect it is very interesting to note that an academic review that Etzioni edited for many years was entitled precisely *The Responsive Commu-nity*, the community that responds, the community that takes responsibility and assumes its duties. Let us try to make this clearer and more verifiable by elucidating on the practical effects of what we have called moral sociology (not social morality).

Moral sociology, as we have seen, from the analytical and proposition-al point of view focuses on the *structures of virtue* and on the *social virtues*, centered on doing, to go to an idea of progress or moral improvement. The proposal of understanding that we make is a new synthesis, a new moral sense centered on having sufficient social sense to act and judge rationally well under the gaze of God. We do not believe that one can speak of moral-ity without an idea of good that is external and somehow permanent. The proposal of moral sociology is centered on the capacity for discernment to look at and improve the structures of virtue and, consequently, to bring to light virtues that, insofar as they respond to the needs of these structures, make us point toward a better life with criteria of benevolence.

For this discourse, we have taken food from some authors who have seemed to us particularly relevant. We pointed to the contributions of Hans Jonas in 1971, those of Amitai Etzioni in 1988, recently also those of Javier Gomá in 2010, and we may add those of Alice von Hildebrand in 2001, but above all, as we mentioned in the first part, those of St. John Paul II in 1987 (*Sollicitudo Rei Socialis*), when he surprised the intellectual world and the Catholic world in general with his concept of *structures of sin*.

In this chapter we are going to speak again mainly of structures of virtue and virtues as cultural and social supports that allow and facilitate a morality of benevolence that becomes present through social acts and individual actions forming good operative charisms. There are many types of structures of virtue just as there are many structures of sin. When one thinks of the structures of sin or the structures of evil, perhaps what comes up the most, what can be linked the most, is the underworld, the terrorist group. Some people say the market, but the market is not a structure of evil. But let's go with what we are talking about, which are the structures of virtue or virtuous social structures that I have divided into four main types.

The *first* of them would be the socially rooted institutions that are born of the society in which they are and that propose to those who live in that society and to those who observe it from outside something virtuous and positive. These institutions may be churches, they may be a fair and orderly market, they may be various systems of voluntary citizen participation of a political, civil, or business nature, they may be corporations that regulate, monitor, promote, or shape both professions and labor associations, and so on. They are entrenched institutions that are there before one is born and will be there afterward. We will try to improve them, it is assumed, but the fact that they precede us and continue gives us a guarantee of their value.

We can also speak, *secondly*, of established and rooted customs that denote and give a certain type of identity and charisma to the society in which they are implanted. These customs can be festive celebrations or details and forms of civility and respect that are transmitted through tradition and the family, such as, among others: the promotion of thrift, industriousness, care for nature, responsible subsidiarity; not to accumulate power but to transfer it as soon as possible to societies, groups, and people who are closer to the ground and who can play their proactive and educational role of good life.

Thirdly, within the structures of virtue, we can also speak of collective defenses that are assumed and, to a certain extent, also enacted, such as the defense of fame, the defense of privacy, the promotion of the critical spirit, the vigilance and defense of human rights and duties, and the proposal of creativity, something that has much to do with the ways in which future generations are educated and that shape the character of people and their own culture.

And *finally*, social structures, which are shared loves and beliefs, somehow vertebrated in the society concerned: the love of children and the family, the protagonism of children and that the laws count on them, the love of tranquility and silence, of gratuity, the promotion of science and the arts, and the care of traditions—all traces that, to the extent that they are shared, generalized, and also vertebrated, make and shape a social fabric characteristic of a place, of a time, and of a people and, with many other structures, trace the identity foundation of a society.

Naturally, we are looking at society from above, and we are seeing social acts, the protagonism of the collective group. But we can also see society from below, from the point of view of individuals. There we must talk about virtues, because virtue structures are nothing without the virtues that are incorporated into human acts. We understand virtue here not as the classics understood it but as habits that promote service and do good outside of oneself. It is, we might say, the social sense of virtue that interests us, a virtue that does good to a who that is not the subject who bears it. Virtue thus understood requires a proposal of fields in which it can be applied.

We could distinguish three fields of operability of virtues: care for others, the commitment to human dignity, and perfectibility. To care is to bet on everything that has to do with human dignity and can contribute to making others better. Speaking first of the virtues of caring, we understand that they are dispositions such as solidarity, respect, exemplarity, defense of others (more than self-defense), mutual help, and security (giving security to others), all of which makes one open to welcome. It is that phrase already mentioned: not if I am my brother's keeper, but if I am my brother's caretaker. The virtues that care are virtues of one toward another, concrete other.

In the second field is dignity, which is a capacity. The virtues of dignity are capacities that are put in place that range from the operational proposal of self-management and self-mastery to autonomy, inner and outer beauty insofar as it can contribute to making it nice to be with someone. This implies hygiene, cleanliness, and religiosity, which influence treatment, or the love of culture, order, etc. They are transcripts that give dignity to others and in the way in which we procure that dignity we exercise some concrete virtues.

And in the third field we had mentioned perfectibility; these are proposed and shared desires that make us a little better to the extent that there is more benevolence in giving than in receiving. Giving improves both parts of sender and receiver and makes others better. There is the love of freedom, the love of plurality, which is a consequence of the previous one, the proposals of equity, hospitality, the same piety that constitutes a reverential attitude toward others, the love of nature and the care of the environment, the promotion of art, the care of festivities or the common heritage of words.

If a person, in these three aspects of care, dignity, and perfectibility, puts his or her potentialities to work, he or she is performing necessary functions that not only benefit individual persons but also raise the moral level of a society. This conjunction of structures of virtue and virtues from the social perspective raises the moral level of an environment. We are talking about a series of analytical proposals that can be made from moral sociology for a better life, and here we have them. Society is a learning community. We have an idea of good that is external to us, but we are creative; new initiatives of progress appear, and we invent things. We also invent systems of living, of sharing, and all of this challenges us. We ought to make an experiential judgment about whether it is on the path of good or, on the contrary, it is on the path of evil.

As a result, we must always be learning. A virtuous morality, we think, is centered on doing, and I believe that the structures of virtue that we have pointed out and also the virtues go that way: in doing, in giving, in always taking others into account, because therein lies our human radicality. We have said many times that we are not social by decision, we are not family by decision or choice, it is something that is given to us: we were born in societies that already exist, in families that already exist, in languages that already exist, and all this makes us see that we should have an attitude of gratitude, of openness, of welcome. Rather than rejection, discarding, or exclusion, morality goes that way. It is the implication between the social act and morality, between sociology and morality, where it seems to me that it is necessary to weave a symbiosis so that our life in common can be a more dignified and ultimately more human life.

I think we are making our way with this proposal that we call moral sociology, but there are still some loose ends to shore up the foundation against the disbelief of the classics with the sociological perspective, because if one speaks of good and evil, how do you base the distinction? We noted before that we are committed to the foundation of morality by means of the criterion of transubjectivity to then arrive at the concept of progress. Human morality and social and human progress are compatible. It is precisely in this measure that we reach the desirable future.

I usually say that morality should not be adjectivized. There are not different morals but one moral, and the qualifier, the adjective proper that it has, is that of human morality. There are people who say, "Well, there is a Christian morality, there is a Buddhist morality, there is an Islamic morality . . ." I think not. There is a human morality, and there is a Christian understanding, a Buddhist understanding, etc. of that morality. If there is a good, there is a morality, and when it comes to seeing the foundations of this morality, we will propose an adequate discernment of moral acts according to our own categories based on precise reasoning. Here I am going to put mine in accordance with what has been exposed so far, so this will give us the opportunity, and this is the reason we are making this exposition, to speak of progress.

When we refer to morality, what we are fundamentally referring to is to do good and avoid evil, and this on the part of both the personal subject and the collective subject, the social subject. How does this, we could say, moral attitude arise in us, what is the synderesis we are referring to? Well, it arises through discursive reason, and I believe that here there are many more agreements than one could imagine. I believe that we are now able to make an integrating effort so that discursive reason, deliberative reason, can illuminate with a little more strength and intensity that adjective we have given to morality, which is human. This integrating effort can now be made more easily than it was many years ago. It is a matter of bringing culture, nature, and reason to the table, and there is a way of doing it, at least the one that I like to defend again, which is based on *transsubjectivity*.

This is that little word that the French sociologist Raymond Boudon planted in current thought and is based on two main premises, as we remember from the previous part. The first is that there is not so much difference when it comes to studying moral truths and so-called positive truths. We already knew this, but we had not paid much attention to what, on the one hand, Simmel had told us—that both positive knowledge and normative knowledge have the same logical legitimization and the same circular process of continuous verification—and, on the other hand, what Popper told us—that all positive or normative knowledge is provisional without ceasing to be objective knowledge. Well, there is not much difference, as Boudon reminds us, between positive truths and moral truths. We are talking about the fact that the force that sustains moral sentiments is proportional to the force of the reasoning on which they are based. That is, if the reasonings by which I have certain moral sentiments can be shared with whomever I want, based on those reasonings that merit objectivity, we can conclude that there is also a kind of moral objectivity.

This is easy to say but sometimes not very easy to explain. To provide an example to my students in class, I propose the case of soccer. Without saying which one, I tell them I can propose a moral truth in soccer: I know which is the best soccer club in the Spanish league. What is more, I am willing to demonstrate it to whoever wants, and that demonstration is not based on my subjectivity but on reasons that I believe will be shared by all, merits through which we can conclude who is, in fact, the best team. If the reasoning is based on good reasons, the moral judgment is the same.

Transsubjectivity does not go against objectivity. Transsubjectivity positions itself against subjectivist relativism insofar as reason is decanted by its weight. At the same time, it is something that is not labeled as perennial because historical progress, if it is given, rides on the conformation of new reasonings that can discard other previous ones. This is where change fits in, which is what sociologists study. Transsubjectivity fundamentally tells us two things. First, that morality is normative, that is, that moral absolutes exist because we can theoretically make the distinction between value and counter-value in the same way as between reason and unreason, and, second, because we can establish hierarchies of values, moral hierarchies, and, consequently, we can speak of moral progress. Morality is normative and morality is perfective.

Morality is, in the latter sense, a collective health that can be measured. Everything that is perfective is measurable; therefore, it is something about which it is possible to make some kind of proposition. The proposal of transsubjectivity is the best foundation we have so far to articulate a morality that sustains the idea of progress. We are history, and for this reason we can establish exchanges of reasoning, megalogues, through time, something that Etzioni told us about. With good reasons at hand, we can see that the norm does not impose itself on reason and that the norm does not impose itself on time. That is not to say that norms should not exist, but rather that they should be reasonable.

Boudon, speaking of transsubjectivity, will tell us that the affections have a rational dimension. Curiously enough, the work in which Boudon exposes his transsubjectivity was published in 1995, the same year in which Spanish philosopher Julián Marías published a book called *Tratado de lo mejor* (*Treatise on the Best*), which seems to me to be very appropriate for the subject we are dealing with, in which philosophy pays particular attention to the social subject in order to propose a morality in which it is also possible to speak of (social) progress. Progress is possible only if we distinguish between the best and the worst, only if we can compare, and thus progress is compatible with morality.

This may attract the attention of those who have dedicated themselves to morality and ethics in a classical sense, but we are proposing an alternative foundation of moral criteria based on the concept of transsubjectivity, which will allow us to speak of the idea of progress and which seems to us to be more accurate than the one we have used up to now. Progress must be stripped of all dogmatism. We sociologists measure progress by default and *a posteriori*. This explains why we have said that morality is perfective because it is a health that can be measured, which is the same thing that doctors do when they measure health by default. What they detect is not health but disease once it has manifested itself (we will return to this in another chapter). There are many ways of being healthy and there is much progress that we do not know and will not know how to catalog until history renders its judgment, i.e., very much *a posteriori*.

The measurement of progress gives us some knowledge, to a certain extent operational, but it does not give us a definitive certainty, and it is true that the certainty we are proposing for morality is not as definitive as that which can be proposed from other conceptual paradigms. But we understand that it is the most logical and the one that best fits with the reality of things and, above all, with social reality. The argument of trans-subjectivity is a rationalist argument, in our opinion superior to behaviorism, to relativism, to the categorical imperative, to hard naturalism and to naturalism, although it has something to do with soft naturalism.

It is a little word I like, transsubjectivity (thank you Boudon). We do not demolish objectivities, we do not go against moral absolutes; rather, we defend them, clarifying that they must be contextualized and that we must erase the label of "perennially" that some people give them. It is possible to speak of progress, it is possible to speak of moral progress, and it is possible to speak of progress in almost everything, and this is the cornerstone of what we say in this book. It is also, in my opinion, the cornerstone on which the social sciences in general and sociology in particular are based. We sociologists study change, although we do not necessarily say that all change tends to progress. The distinction is often made between progressivism or conservatism, but there is a third possibility. Certain progressives often ignore that the alternative to progress is decadence, immobility (conservatism) is there but when one moves one can move in two directions: toward progress or toward decadence, something to keep in mind.

Well, leaving aside the fundamentals, it remains, to end the chapter, to enter into the hierarchy of values. Thus, we will end up defending a civility of maximums and a government of minimums as an expression of optimal morality. Let's go there.

The modern understanding of equality is deficient. We highlight a paradox: for equality, both hierarchy and estrangement are necessary. At the same time, we note that, in according with the matter spoken about in the first part, the absence of hierarchy and the absence of strangeness necessarily lead to fragmentation and inequality.

Language sometimes confuses us because at times we use the same terms to describe values and to speak of virtues. Values have much to do with virtues, but there is also a need to mark the differences. Values are rather, as we know, of conceptual roots; they are ideas applied to ends and means for the achievement of undertakings, social processes, and situations that are considered more or less optimal. Virtues, on the contrary, are operationally embodied, present in the subjects that supposedly carry out, propose, or discover virtuous actions. Virtues, while acting outside the subject, are embedded in us, while values, on the other hand, are more theoretical.

Referring now to values, the analysis we wish to make is more comprehensive if we begin to speak of hierarchy. What we are going to remember is that without a hierarchy of values, equality cannot be preached. Therefore, if we defend equality, we must also defend hierarchy. The corollary is that some values are more important than others and, therefore, some societies are better than others. Otherwise, they could not be measured or compared, and sociologists are dedicated to comparing by measuring. Although it is very difficult to measure qualities and much easier to measure quantities, sometimes we get carried away by the euphoria of quantity, qualities must also be measured.

We start from the premise that to measure supposedly qualifiable quality values, what we should do first is to put them in context. Not all values are worth the same in different contexts and not all are worth the same in what can be universalized. That is why we proposed that scale in four steps: basic values or being, central values or feeling, substantive values or thinking, and expressive values or doing. However, these and other breakdowns and scales of values and virtues, which had their heyday, may no longer be much in vogue at this moment. Now, the goal seems to be conceptual consolidation trying to bring together what matters into overarching ideas. And in this, there seems to be a kind of struggle, a "moral wrestling," as Etzioni puts it in *The Moral Wrestler* (*Society*, 2017), aiming to summarize rather than dissect moral virtues into mono-concepts. For example, *homo economicus* for many economists, genetics for social biologists, relativism for cultural anthropologists, heredity traces for clinical psychologists, or narratives for social psychologists. All these concepts fall short because they leave us without the firm moral ground provided by those other personal and collective virtues that we tried to differentiate and put in order hierarchically. It is no surprise, then, that Etzioni concludes the wrestling by saying: *"It seems that the place to look for new grounds on which to understand the forces that can make us better may be either in modern religions or in other forms of spirituality and transcendentalism, and in the works of those individual social scientists who do not conform to the norms of their disciplines."*

What we are saying here has to do with the game of disciplines. One argues and speaks from sociology and, well, here there is sociology but there is also politics, government action or governance, and public morality. There is relationship and implication even from different epistemological presuppositions. A phrase that I like to repeat a lot is that maximum civility is parallel to minimum government. If we want government to be minimal in the sense that it is better, that the less things government takes care of the better, it will be a sign that its citizens are responsible enough to take care of everything else. Then there will be hierarchical balance and there can be social progress. Progress rides on the virtues and values assumed personally and collectively, not only, as a certain point of view thinks, by those assumed by a government.

For this to be possible, it is necessary that we have clear criteria on the hierarchy of values and on the distinction of opposites both in values and virtues. This seems elementary. In the same way that we make that distinction, we also should make another very necessary one in this respect. It is between the criteria of work and research when comparing and measuring that we could label as empirical logical criteria and affective normative criteria.

Relevant here are the intervention and contributions of Etzioni, who says that the distinction often made in the social sciences between feelings and reason is too artificial. It is true that feelings are rational, they have a rational component, and that reason cannot be separated from feelings because every rational choice is preceded by a sentimental choice. We choose to study something, we choose to look at something, because there is something inside us that moves us to do so. Well, if we do not separate logical-empirical reasoning from normative-affective reasoning, then we will not be able to realize that when measuring we must also consider the collective; that is, we must consider the weight of the social in individual decisions and opinions.

Here it is usually economic science that is lacking, which unfortunately forgets normative-affective criteria when it comes to making measurements and comparisons and focuses too much on logical-empirical criteria. Thus, to measure growth and identify it with development, we cannot have this fixation. That is why we said that the primary use of the perceptual increase in annual GDP when comparing countries, when social health leads us to think that there are much more important things, is dysfunctional. True progress is moral progress and GDP may have something to do with it, but composing hierarchies of countries according to logical-empirical economic criteria only leads to confusion. To compare and propose equality, it is important to take a walk through the hierarchy. To the extent that we are clear about this hierarchy, we will be able to feel equal and part of a self-conscious civility. We will also be able to feel part of the different communities to which at the same time we belong, sharing basic moral codes.

Some people think that morality is something to be studied by theologians, that it is for believers, or that morality is to comply with the law. No, morality is superior to positive law (justice is superior to law, jurists say), it is what governs or should govern our lives. Morality allows us to speak as human beings to the point that its proper qualifier is "human." The sciences should allow us to recognize the value of morality and not look the other way as if it did not go beyond the law. From our balcony, sociology should help us to understand morality, economics, politics, and of course philosophy. But here we have looked at the intimate and fundamental relationship between sociology or the methodology of sociology and the moral proposal. We believe it is a relationship that is open to fructify in many academic endeavors, and that is why we have proposed what we have called, as a new approach, moral sociology. We think that without it as a starting point there is no society to come that is worthwhile.

4. The Real Economy

THERE IS AN INTIMATE relationship between political freedom and economic freedom, and the connivance between both freedoms requires making a double distinction: between market and gift on the one hand and between profit and service on the other. As on many occasions, we should refer to grammar, to language, and specifically to names and adjectives because, speaking of the relationship between economy and society, many names have been used and invented lately. Thus, we have ecology, ecosophy, socioeconomics, and also eco-sociology that speak, or try to speak, from economic presuppositions. Behind all these new nomenclatures there are basic concepts that have been discussed and which, when reflecting on the subject, must be brought up.

Undoubtedly, the most important is that of freedom. Many labels can be given to freedom, but, as I have always tried to remember, with the qualifier human, all others are superfluous. Nevertheless, to clarify, we will refer to at least two of these adjectives. But before doing so, to show how difficult it is to reach an agreement on what freedom is, let us mention some of its definers. If we recall, Friedrich Hayek distinguishes between freedom and liberties; Isaiah Berlin distinguishes between positive freedom and negative freedom; some of those trained in the health sciences distinguish between internal freedom and external freedom; we have suggested that it is good to ask ourselves about what freedom, from what freedom, for what freedom, from whom freedom, and even against whom; but, in the end, what we have proposed, on more than one occasion, is the convenience of understanding freedom as self-possession, as self-mastery, a dominion that necessarily excludes the dominion of others: both that others dominate me and that I dominate others. Freedom understood as self-possession necessarily implies responsibility. One is free to the extent of one's responsibility, so if we want to be freer, we must be more responsible.

But to explain what we mean by freedom as self-possession and self-mastery, the difference between Freedom with a capital letter F and freedom with a small letter f, as we have also stated in some other texts, we should ask ourselves whether it is conceivable that with the deprivation of freedoms one can be free. The answer we have given is yes, and we propose for the consideration of this answer the ideal type of the prisoner who is his own master. A person who is a prisoner but who owns himself is a person who has freedom with a capital letter even if he does not have freedom with a small letter, a person who has criticism, who has culture, who has religion, who has vital sustenance, and who has health is free with a capital letter even if he is not free with a small letter, understanding that what is really important is freedom with a capital letter. But the prisoner who is not his own master is not free in any way, the prisoner who is tortured, the prisoner who is deprived of vital sustenance, the prisoner who is pharmacologically manipulated, the prisoner who is induced to a mental dependence, and the prisoner who is not entirely rational, that prisoner is not free in any way.

We said before that we do not like the qualifiers of these great concepts, and one of them is freedom. As we pointed out, neither is that of morality, but for pedagogical reasons we are going to adjective two here: economic freedom and political freedom. I have taught the discipline of sociology for many years in a faculty of economics; therefore, I think I know what most economists think. Too many times, freedom has been explained as a consequence of economic freedom. It has been explained in such a way that the founding fathers of freedom seem to be those egregious economists who are called classics and among whom Adam Smith is included. Market freedom is what, according to them, would later introduce us to political freedoms. Thus, we would go from freedom with a small letter to freedom with a capital letter. I am of the opinion that, with apologies to those distinguished economists, it is the other way around. Freedom with a capital letter comes first, political freedom and all that follows from it, then comes economic freedom, the market strictly speaking. If we affirm that first comes freedom with a capital letter, political freedom, we will necessarily refer to the School of Salamanca. Thus, there are those who have studied the relationship between Luis de Molina and Hayek, arguing for economic freedoms based on more basic freedoms.

I have made this introductory parenthesis on how one understands freedom and how difficult it is to agree on what it consists of and what the types of freedom are, in order to go now to the subject that motivates this chapter, which is the real economy. The first two points we want to touch on are two distinctions that, in my opinion, are important. The first is between market and gift, and here we advocate a strict conceptual separation to make the market compatible with the gift and, at the same time, to make them distinguishable. Mercantilists tend to consider that the gift is part of the market on the understanding that the gift is a kind of market transaction that protects freedoms and, therefore, can be incorporated into the market. This is the view of some Nobel Prize winners in economics, such as Gary Becker. Consequently, if the gift is part of the market, in the end we realize that we include people in the market as objects (ultimately identifying a gift time that is worth zero together with other mercantile times that are worth money). But no, the gift is not part of the market although it influences it. Here, what we are going to try to do is to constrain the market a little because mercantilism has exaggerated it to the point of making it almost comparable to society, and that is a major mistake.

The market has its place, and the gift has its other "place." We put place in quotation marks because we are not referring to spaces but to times and modes of relationship. We are not talking about spatial places, about what we see in a building that says "market" on it, no. We are referring to modes of relationship between people, between individuals, and between communities. The economy goes much further than the market because the economy must also study the gift apart from the merchandise. It will be easy to see that a gift affects many economic factors, including prices, wages, securities, and property. Therefore, it is something that economists and economics should study, but as something different from the market.

To distinguish between monetary and non-monetary economy, that is, to distinguish between profit and service, is the second point of our consideration. There is an implication here that we feel is necessary to emphasize. Money and service are mutually implicated (also genealogically). We will hardly be able to donate if we do not have, and this having can be the fruit of profit, but it is also difficult for us to intervene in the market if we have not first received donations. Those donations operate fundamentally in the domestic economy and not in the mercantile economy and enable us to intervene in the market as human beings, as free subjects. There is a need to involve and link profit and service, even though they are different. Without profit it is difficult to have service, but without service it is impossible to have profit.

We must consider, on the other hand, that a great part of human transactions take place in the sphere of the family, and the greater part of the transactions refer to gift, to service. They are not mercantile transactions. Parents and children interact economically outside the market, and that economy is a basic economy, a fundamental economy, a backbone economy that gives us freedom with capital letters. Freedom with small letters can be given to us both by the market and by the surrounding liberality. Freedom with a capital letter makes us human, it comes from our humanity that has been shaped in our familiar radicality, and freedom with a lower case is something that we can exercise thanks, among other things, to the market. The two, the market and the gift, profit and service, are necessary, distinguishable, and compatible.

I believe that we must break a lance here in defense, at least among those of us who have criticized capitalism, and above all financial capitalism, in defense, we say, of the market. The market is necessary. Without the market there is no viable society, and profit is one of the consequences of participating in the market. At the same time, we must pay attention to the fact that the market is only one of the three legs of the table, as our admired Amitai Etzioni used to say: state, market, and community sustain society. That is why, in our work, we have advocated an alliance between state and community that puts the market in its place.

We are talking about constraining the market. We are advocating that the economy be more concerned with the gift, that it be more concerned with presents, and all of that happens outside the market. And while it is good that there are economists specialized in market issues, it is now much more necessary that there are also economists specialized in the gift economy, in the economy of service, and in the economy of presents. They are two different realities that imply and need each other. These two realities, gift and market, need to live in peace and need to have equality between them, to be treated with the same attention, and today, unfortunately, they are not. At a time when consumerism, materialism, and ambition for power prevail, the market has supplanted almost everything and has included us all, even us as members of family subjects that operate without markets, within the market. It has turned us into products, and that is called, in my opinion, exploitation.

Reflecting now on globalization, the family, and power from the economic sphere, we stress the need for a coherent critique of financial capitalism based on a conception of the family as a productive unit of intangibles and a revaluation of service. This will allow us to complete the picture, beyond what has been said, of what we call the real economy.

In our opinion, the three points that remain to be dealt with in the economic sphere if we are to lay the foundations for a better future are those that deal with globalization, the family, and power. We are using the adjective "real" because the economy that is often presented to us by the media and the economy that many economists deal with is only half of it. It is the monetary economy, the economy of material goods, which, as we are saying, is not taken into account, or is not taken into account as much as it should be, the non-monetary economy, the economy of immaterial goods that aim at moral purposes.

But let us get down to business. The first of the points raised is globalization. We refer to the globalization of capital, to what has also been called financial capitalism, and the first observation we bring up is how it is possible for capital to have more rights than people. Capital circulates throughout the world with practically no restrictions, often without oversight, something that people cannot do, and somehow gives capital advantages over labor and those who provide it, which produce defects and problems that point to a scourge: the scourge of exploitation. Even when this exploitation is not perceived as such, the relationship between the globalization of capital and exploitation is manifested when we discern who benefits from the globalization of capital and who is harmed by it.

If we think about it, there are three groups of people who receive the greatest benefit from the globalization of capital. On the one hand, there are the traffickers. I say traffickers because, in my opinion, they deserve the same amoral category as those who engage in human trafficking. In effect, they produce the same thing. They are the speculators and intermediaries in the movement of capital with the buying and selling of assets on the world's stock exchanges. On the other hand, there are the power elites in countries that directly or indirectly advocate what has come to be called state capitalism. The power elites manage capital without any type of control and, at the same time, manage people inside and outside their areas of power. In third place, without trying to be exhaustive, we can put the rentiers, those great world fortunes that manage capital sums larger than those of many countries. They manage without having the slightest knowledge of the effect this management has on the people. The management of capital is often done for speculative purposes, others for directly perverse purposes, such as the annulment of a contrary. This affects many people who lose their jobs, companies that are destroyed or closed arbitrarily, only benefiting, apart from those mentioned above, anonymous investors whose fortunes are not known and who operate through what are called investment funds or venture capital funds. Here, it is said, capitalists gamble their money, but it is not said that in this game there are collateral victims that have nothing to do with global finance.

Apart from those mentioned above, this group of beneficiaries includes the mass of large and medium-sized fortunes, which can hardly be considered directly involved in the global movement of capital but, in many cases, engage in stock market speculation or try to jump on the bandwagon of digital or communications monopolies that often violate the laws that prevent them from doing so in many countries. Today, the possibilities of investor choice are mostly configured from a single ownership vertex that offers the maximum possible range of activities. Macro-conglomerates that cover from opposite ideological extremes (this is very common in communication groups) to complete manufacturing sectors with monopolistic aspirations, always on the lookout for speculative sales and purchases. Capital, they say, is made to roll.

But in addition to all these, perhaps the largest group of benefactors is made up of naive people, mostly citizens of rich countries, who, driven by compulsive consumerism, buy cheap products without knowing that this purchase is in some way facilitated by the exploitation of slave labor, and even child labor, in poor countries where human rights are perhaps not respected, much less international labor laws. The damage they do is twofold. You earn that cheap product compared to the same product at a higher price without realizing that you are not only facilitating that exploitation, where labor is cheap, but also harming the labor that has struggled for years to get a good wage, to have its hours respected, and to have human rights enforced in your country so that the dignity of the worker is in accordance with the requirements of justice and the law.

A characteristic of the globalization of financial capitalism is its performative impulse. This contrasts it with the family. The family has or should have a personhood insofar as it is an economic and civil subject. But the family is also the factory and workshop of personality in the sense that it is through the family that people are produced who are capable of operating in the market in the right way. The family as a person and the family as a factory of persons is conceptually opposed to the personalization of capital, which claims and obtains more and more rights in the hope of transforming individuals into compulsive consumers. There is here a perverse alliance that it is convenient to denounce, and it is the alliance between capital and power. An alliance that is often directed precisely against the family. We remember Hannah Arendt, when speaking of totalitarianism, said that to achieve the submission of many, there is nothing easier than to separate individuals from their group.

The family (to which we will dedicate a chapter later) is, among other things, a unit of production, a productive subject. Naturally, we are referring to a unit of production of immaterial goods, of intangible goods, which are very important from the point of view of the morality of a society. And perhaps they are so important that, therefore, attention should be paid to them, and they should be very present in the economic discourse. The injection of morality that the family as a productive subject gives and donates to society is very necessary because if the current economy is lacking in anything, it is precisely morality. The insertion of morality given by the family has a lot to do with the need to dematerialize the economy.

There is much talk nowadays that, due to the ecological crisis, perhaps one of the most important economic problems is not to ensure growth but to propose an orderly and acceptable degrowth. I think that before proposing this degrowth, it may be necessary to emphasize and pay attention to the need to dematerialize the economy, to put welfare and well-being on a par. The economy should not only aim at rationalizing trade and the production of material goods but also strive to rationalize the production of immaterial goods.

With dematerialization we would all win because, among other things, the training as persons that the family provides is something necessary for the market and necessary for politics. Thinking that this training is done person to person, collective or individual, the collective person that is the family and the individual person that is each one of us, there is a conscience of self-possession and self-mastery that characterizes the personal being that will help both the state and the market provide an affordable transition. That is why this perverse alliance between power and capital, which, as we have mentioned, results in corruption, should become an alliance of excellence between the state and the family to put capital in its place. And to put the market in its place as well, a place not only smaller from the point of view of the material economy but also much wider from the point of view of the economy of nonmaterial goods.

The economy of non-monetary goods touches on the issue of power. In our opinion, power and its political game of excessive ambitions is what clouds any future. Power is the great disturber, the great corrupter. Full freedom is incompatible with power because, among other things, the antithesis of power is service, and service is something that operates fundamentally in non-political spheres, such as the domestic sphere. But we would try to replicate it and take it out of there so that it also operates in the political sphere; the objective of politicians should be to serve the citizenry, not to benefit from it. There is a pertinent reflection to be made here on the injection of morality we spoke of earlier. The globalization of capital, as we have seen, has not led to a globalization of dignity, which is what it was all about, but we do think that freedom is an immaterial good that has material consequences. Freedom is something that can be fostered more in the family than in power, and that is why we advocate, as we will see later, that many of the competencies of the established powers, specifically the state, should be addressed in the future by the family.

We refer mainly to education, to communal self-management, to neighborhood security, and to the excellence that should be given to community services. We remember that criticism made by the Romans themselves about how the spirit of the republic had been forgotten or perverted, and the answer was that it had been perverted because the service to the commons had been neglected in favor of the private. When families, as environments of service and gift, take charge of the commons, then the levels of excellence of the public will rise to the extent that the family is more capable than the state to take care of things that are closer to it and to the extent that monetary investment is replaced by service work. Likewise, there is a factor to be recognized here, and that is that while the monetary economy operates with scarce products, since supply and demand play an important role in the issue of scarcity, the non-monetary economy operates with products that are or can be considered infinite. We are speaking specifically of service, which is precisely the opposite, as we have said, of power.

A derivative and interesting topic is the relationship that the economy has with happiness. We know what the classics said about maximum happiness for the maximum possible number of people. Well, service contributes more to happiness than power. It is also common sense: the reality of happiness is expansive, and that happiness would be a little more assured to the extent that we managed to dissociate power from freedom. Not to put them as a zero-sum product: where there is more power there is less freedom and where there is more freedom there is less power. That is where love must come in, where service has to come in. We have seen before that we can be free without power in the figure of the ideal type of the self-possessed prisoner. We can also be very happy without power if that happiness is achieved through service. We should give a channel to service so that it is present and considered as a very important part of the real economy. Unfortunately, this is not being done now.

This is particularly relevant for the times in which we live because the great problems of humanity today are very much related to politics and economics. It is a pity that when we look at the reality of life we do not incorporate, both in politics and economics, what really matters and what we radically are. We are family beings—we care about being loved, and we care about service—so let's bet on the family. Let's bet on recognizing ourselves as debtors of love, let's bet on cooperation instead of competitiveness, and let's incorporate all this into the economic discourse that is running out of moral steam.

5. Fear

Social fear produces the submission of the masses, a new and current phenomenon that denounces the lack of courage in the collective subject. We are waiting for some emotional spark to awaken us so that freedom may vivify our social being. There is much fear and insecurity, and this makes human collectivities docile and submissive.

Social fear is a recurrent theme in sociological thought as well as philosophy. It is, we could say, the determining factor in today's culture. There is something characteristic of today's culture and that is that fear is understood in a different way than it has been understood until now. Fear has always been a fear of the strong or a fear of the equal. Fear of the equal was Thomas Hobbes's contribution in *Leviathan*. The British philosopher postulated as early as 1651 that it is fear that makes the state possible (and necessary). We are all equally vulnerable; therefore, we are all "dangerous." Rather than fear, Durkheim would speak of social anguish. He said that it was the transformation of external coercion into internal coercion. Michel Foucault extracted from this that fear inclines men positively and rationally to invent the leviathan. It was like the invisibilities of a continuous and perpetual war.

Germanic thinkers are perhaps those who have studied fear the most, and among them, fundamentally, is Norbert Elias, who spoke of *homo clausus*, of the solitude of man locked up in himself. Elias told us that fear was an unintended effect of historical change: it was the material from which social opacity was made. Ulrich Beck came later to postulate the risk society. Here, many understood the risk as external. Thus, much in the same way as the externalities in the market economy, our culture is producing fear. A fear that is digestible and that accumulates an ever-increasing risk for a future that is feared. The Spaniard Gil Calvo, based on Beck's contributions, said that fear is the message: it is the message and heritage of our culture. German-Korean thinker Byung-Chul Han concludes that the problem is a permanent self-exploitation that is the self-deception in which we are immersed to, at the same time, feed our fear and produce it in others.

Fear is a subject that has almost always been talked about, but now it is treated in a peculiar way. In the analysis of fear in the present time there is something fundamentally different, and that is the response to that fear. Previously, it had been said that fear produced the city. The city was studied as an area of security that protected from the dangerous rural and wild weather. The walled city was thus a symbol of strength. Now, however, today's city is presented to us as an area of insecurity where fear is produced by super specialization, a consequence of modernity. Super specialization makes each of us more dependent on others, and dependence, which is seen as the antithesis of the deception of autonomy, creates insecurity. We do not trust each other, and we need a guarantor, a strong power that makes us trust each other under that guarantee and surveillance. This produces a kind of Stockholm syndrome, which makes us feel comfortable in fear. We tolerate it because the state gives us a supposed security that we can see and feel in the structures of defense and coercion.

It is a way of explaining modern fear in a theoretical sense, so to speak, but in this end of modernity, fear has produced a different and peculiar effect, something that characterizes us and was unthinkable before. It is the submission of the masses. We have gone from the revolt or revolution of the masses to the opposite, the submission of the masses. The answer to fear is no longer to break with nothing but to continue doing the same thing with pity. It is self-censorship; we do not want to change things because we cannot trust ourselves. We have gone from a fear of doing to a fear of suffering. We are condemned to suffer, and in order not to make it worse, the answer to fear is now submission. A collective submission compatible with individual insubordination.

The protagonism of the mass here is a protagonism by default. It is like the paralysis produced by someone that neither goes nor lets anybody go. At the same time, the mass that we are seems indispensable to us to overcome the dangers that are foreseen in the future and makes us insensitive to overcome the shortcomings of the present. It condemns us to perpetual fear. Collectively, we have become cowards as we have never been cowards before. We have never had more power over us, more instruments of security, and yet never before have we found ourselves, willingly, in a situation of helplessness and dispossession, in a situation, some would say, of slavery. Collectively, the social subject thinks of himself as incapable and hopeless. It is not anomie, and it is not Marxist alienation; it is the current timidity. We have grown old. We see ourselves without value in both senses of the word, value without courage and without merit. Collectively speaking, from the submission of the masses, we have passed to a submissive and resigned society: to structural and social fear.

How did we get into this situation? What happened to us? We can review a few factors that may help our analysis. In the first place, punishment. The submission of the masses is guaranteed by the great penalties for insubordination. An insubordination that is punished by ostracism, but an ostracism that threatens where there is no possible exile, there is no America to go to, there is no place to go into exile. That ostracism is something like suddenly being locked into nothingness, and that gives us more panic than death. That is why someone has said that if before fear was a fear of death, now fear is a fear of life.

Timidity can also be the result of a lack of courage, of the little importance and specific weight we give to courage. Courage is no longer admired, and collective courage is labeled as dangerous. Courage is nowadays a provocation, a dysfunction, an extremism. This has something to do with the corrosion of male character and the crisis of masculinity, that excessive eagerness to label attitudes that come from the lack of control of that dangerous element we call masculinity, that we are not taught to educate, as machismo. Nowadays, in times that we qualify as post heroic, men discover their femininity in the same way that women discover their masculinity, and there is tremendous confusion. In this confusion, multiple suspicions are denounced, and one of them precisely concerns courage.

We can also look at the concealment of death. Human sensitivity slips from feeling, which seems to be something positive, to sensation. In mere sensation, death produces negativity; therefore, we ought to hide it. In the collective imaginary we use death as a denunciation, but we do not use death as a question, as something that challenges us, as something of ours and of concrete meaning that sooner or later we will face. Life necessarily implies death. Thus, transhumanism and other fashions of limitless richness, in the height of their overbearing naivety, pretend to skip that implication.

The stigmatization of violence, of any violence, may also be one of the causes of this submission of the masses. Without violence, with pardon, there is no life. Measured violence makes justice survive, because the only way to combat excessive violence is measured violence. There are legitimate forms of violence, such as the violence of defense and, in particular, the violence of the defense of others, of the protection we give to others in any way, personally or institutionally. And there is a duty of care, a duty to welcome, to care for and defend the innocent, a duty of collective responsibility, and in the face of that responsibility we cannot pretend to stigmatize any kind of violence, because sometimes it will be necessary.

There is no insubordination because the deterrence is very strong. It is a dissuasion by estrangement, which is why the single way of thinking reigns supreme. Academic uniformity is thus shaped as endogamy. There is fear of dissent in the face of the threat of cancellation that penalizes those who dare to think differently. In the past, this seemed impossible. The best deterrent force now is not the security forces, the police, but the media, to the point that the stigmatization of a government in the media produces panic because power does not necessarily corrupt anymore. What necessarily corrupts today is the fear of losing it.

How do we overcome this situation, if it is possible to overcome it? How do we declare ourselves socially insubmissive? How can we face this social fear that paralyzes us in the uniformization of the concentration camp? Well, one answer we can give is that this fear cannot be overcome alone. We do not need, as in the past, either heroes, or saints, or ladies and gentlemen who defend their honor at all costs; we need those who are not free either, we need to shape opinion, and we need to identify ourselves collectively with insubordination. We need, in short, to claim a plurality.

Undoubtedly, this will happen. A current of opinion will spread, bringing together the masses, bringing them together socially in cultural alternatives that will allow us to overcome social fear and allow us to dissent. Konrad Lorentz said that a nonrational and emotional factor is always needed to share a rational cognition. René Girard would say that this is precisely a scapegoat, the spark that awakens our slave consciousness and, at the same time, gives us the wings to make insubordination our banner. Humans are insubmissive to the extent that we are free, and where there is no plurality, there is no freedom. Where fear standardizes us all equally there is no freedom, and that is what, in my opinion, is happening now and was not happening before, at least in such a clear way.

The fears of modernity lead to a situation of structural fear that has turned the masses into an inert, docile, and passive subject. Everything is, they say, under control. Dissent is punished. The thought that does not fit with the supposed orthodoxy is persecuted and punished. And it is not punished as the first modernity was punished, the punishment is now conformist in the form of auto penalty. It is we ourselves who punish our capacities, who culturally adapt ourselves so as not to dissent, who censor ourselves into submission.

We must wake up. There will be a spark that wakes us up and we ought to be attentive to that spark that makes light, produces that lightning that moves us inside, and makes us aware that, as humans, without freedom we cannot breathe. There is fear, yes, fear is human too, but the answer to fear is courage. A courage that has here a social claim that implies a link with some in momentary dissonance with others. In any change of epoch, it has happened this way, and this one, I believe, is not going to be less.

6. The Limit

THE CONCEPT OF LIMIT as a channel is a necessary reference to understand the world and our place in it. Discerning the typologies and the obstacles that have the proper understanding of the limit will allow us to enter with a minimum of security and certainty in the configuration of social development proposals that envision a better future.

We try to stay at a conceptual level, and we will ask ourselves, first of all, whether it is reason or the heart that draws the limits that impose conceptual boundaries. Our starting hypothesis is that the heart proposes, but reason disposes. All self-recognition, whether individual or collective, implies a rational exercise. From here we can try to make a division of typologies of limits. We could speak of constitutive limits, unconditioned limits, circumstantial limits, internal limits, or external limits. I like to propose a typology of six types of limits. Following Bauman's adjective of the liquid society, we can speak of solid limits, liquid limits, gaseous limits, provisional limits, false limits, and transitory limits.

The solid limits would be those derived from our given biological or social constitution. Thus, for example, the limits derived from our familiar strangeness, which is something radically human. They must always be considered and are not provisional in nature. In fact, they are written in many countries on the identity card. They condition existence and life in a radical way. Liquid limits, on the other hand, would be those of a cultural nature, for example, languages, although we can also consider some that have a material transcendence, such as inheritances. They limit our relationships and shape our expectations as well as those of others about us. The gaseous limits would be those endowed with a more manifest, perhaps even arbitrary, provisional limit, such as traffic laws, and the empathy we may feel for some people or the antipathy we may feel toward others. Provisional limits are political limits, those that depend on the configuration of power, and technological limits, those that impose on us the provision of gadgets until others arrive. False limits, fifthly, are those that are discovered to be false either by analyzing history with new data, which was hidden or unknown until then, or by investigating the logical proposal that presents them as a limit. Making a bit of a joke, we can name in this category those diets or unfounded beliefs that we discover as such by rational analysis. And then there are, finally, the transitory limits, which are those derived from age or knowledge.

We have done this little tour to show that the limit is not something negative but rather in many cases the other way around. They should not be understood as a negation but as a channel in certain typologies, as an incentive or challenge in others, and as an obstacle—salvageable or not, depending on the circumstances—in others still. The limit of life is death, and the understanding of the limit as negative is something we must reject from the outset, even though there are people who believe themselves to be unlimited or limited only by themselves. In the same way we also reject that limits are decided only by the heart.

The negative conception of the limit is conditioned by one of the basic presuppositions of modern culture, which is autonomy. The evil of autonomy (e.g., I can do it all, I am capable of anything if I set my mind to it), combined with a certain amount of individualism, is antisocial. Society, insofar as it refers us to each other as an organic whole, subject to change, places us in the context that social life is change without ceasing to be social. It is true of mere living. The change of mode, from social to nonsocial, is not a valid way out of the channel. Without conceptual limit there is no self-recognition; I am the other of the other, and there is no distinction of limits without which society would be the uniformity of nothingness. We have limits, and because of these individual and collective limitations there is pluralism and diversity. Consequently, there will be self-recognition and innate and ascribed identities.

However, in the epigones of modern culture there are some traces and understandings that have come to put the concept of the limit between parentheses. To me, they seem to be somewhat negative proposals that do not help us to understand either the time in which we live or who we really are. We are going to list four of these proposals or understandings that, in my opinion, we should overcome in order to properly understand the concept of limit.

The first of these, and this has a fundamental impact on the discipline of economics, is spatial materialization. A judgment that results in a prejudice by identifying space with the object, leaving the subject without place, without conceptual space. By means of this operation, the mercantile economy pretends to detach itself from the borders of concept. Thus, there is no limit for the market: everything is an object, including, unfortunately, some people. This spatial materialization of the economy that pretends to reach all objects—that is, everything—must be overcome, as we have already commented.

The second approach that we should overcome, and which we have just mentioned, is individualism. Individualism disintegrates human groups by depriving them of strangeness, of distinction, and of the defense of identity plurality. To the criticism of the individualists, I must answer that it is true that there are false, illusory, irrational, and even murderous identities, as is explicit in the title of a book, but we must know that without identities we are nobody. We are talking about identities in the plural because each one of us has several. Without identities, we are nobody because we would not be able to distinguish ourselves.

Thirdly, we should overcome the instrumentalization of work. To understand work as something merely instrumental which, consequently, implies that technology becomes an end in itself, is tremendously pernicious. It is the technification of life. On the horizon is that tremendous confusion that we end up confusing our tools and utensils as our long-range external "human" components. Techniques of play that are like our pets, or techniques of domination that procure us slaves. Technology, when it becomes an end in itself, pursued for its own sake, ends up imposing itself on us. Here, many times, the novelty of these gadgets ends up imposing itself on rationality.

The fourth approach to overcome is that fashion of reductionism which focuses on the part and ignores the whole, a fashion derived from the absence of a sociological perspective in contemporary discourse (if there is one). Society is an organic whole, and we cannot understand it as if it were a mechanical apparatus composed of parts. Society is not an aggregate. The predominance of the mechanics of the parts over the dynamics of the forces ends up imposing itself over teleology, over the ends, which end up being ignored. And society, like everything organic, despite so many, has ends.

The proposal to overcome these four understandings in order to see the limit as something positive clashes with the approaches derived from the idealization of the idea of inexorable linear progress. If there are limits, there are channels that, in some way, define us. We have spoken of a typology of limits, some more important than others, but the conjugation of all of them points out to us who we are, which are the paths by which we can reach higher levels of well-being, dignity, justice, and progress. However, when this concept becomes concrete and we come to say this is a limit or this is not a limit, then problems arise.

I would now like to refer to two of them. One is the relationship between limit and fear. When we speak of limit in the abstract, there may not be many fears, but when we concretize that limit, it immediately seems that what we are concretizing is a prize to see who can get closer to the limit without exceeding it. That is crazy. Setting the limit is not a blackjack card game. You don't have to get close to the challenge but let yourself go with the limit and advance along the course without getting out of it. Perhaps this is what Ulrich Beck was referring to when he spoke of the risk society. There is, I don't know why, an eagerness to put oneself at risk to feel unique sensations. Now I remember the adjective that was said about some people: this guy is an edge, as if to say that he is a person who is always bordering on the limit of what is wrong, a person who has a bad idea, who has no criteria and that it would be better to stay far away from him. The limits serve us as a channel, they mark a route for us, not a fence that we must necessarily cross.

The other problem is the relationship between limit and transgression. The concept of limit does not necessarily lead us to say that all transgression is bad because we have seen that there are limits that are false. Even more, some of them need transgression. If we have a provisional limit and we understand it as a solid limit, then someone will come and tell us that we are wrong. The concept of limit does not put a negative label on transgression, which is sometimes very necessary.

There are some authors who have illuminated in a special way the reflection on the limit. I would like to mention that before moving on. The first one who encouraged me to deepen and use this concept in sociology was E. F. Schumacher, the author of *Small Is Beautiful*. In this and other works, Schumacher continually uses the concept of limit to make novel, interesting, and useful proposals, many of which unfortunately have not been put into practice. Also, Marshall Mcluhan and Lewis Mumford, to whom I have returned lately, without forgetting Wendell Berry, Gunther Anders, and, in general, many other authors who label themselves as communitarians. The concept of community itself implies limit—or better, limits—sometimes conveniently superimposed.

In creative literature we can also find the concept of the limit illustrated in concrete lives. One always refers to Cervantes who, like no one else, speaks of the human, making us see the importance of limits and channels. This is not only in his masterpiece *Don Quixote* but also in almost all of his work. Reading Cervantes, one ends up realizing that the concept of limit is very valuable, because one can look for it in the distance without having to realize that one is wrong to cross it. The Spaniards Gabriel Miró and Miguel de Unamuno have also expressed in a somewhat radical way the limit that humanizes and dehumanizes us at the same time, pointing out a contrast between reason and unreason that marks the map of life. And among non-Spanish writers, G. K. Chesterton, of course.

Mention should also be made of those who were grotesquely mistaken when it came to setting limits where there were none and who became famous, such as Paul Ehrlich, author of *The Population Bomb*, and Dennis Meadows, with his book *The Limits to Growth*. Xavier Casp, the great Valencian poet, used to say: "I do not want to climb higher but to go deeper" ("Yo no vull pujar mes alt," 1985). In order to develop, perhaps, we should also look inside ourselves, where there may be far fewer limits than we think.

Notwithstanding all this and what has been said so far, today, the gender issue has taken the debate on limits by storm to the point of almost monopolizing it and, to a certain extent, disturbing it. From our point of view, the issue is cultural and focuses on values. Those which history and our culture have presented to us adjectivally as masculine or feminine. Our position is that such values can be changed, which does not necessarily imply that sexuality has or can be changed as well.

We also want to be precise, trying to make myself understood in a matter where I have failed to do so most of the times I have dealt with this subject. One understands that men and women are neither complementary nor supplementary. In itself, men and women are necessary. It is true that, from a social point of view, old and young, sick and healthy, tall and short, men and women complement each other. It is also true that, in some tasks, learned and unlearned, young and old, men and women can supplement each other, but not so in other tasks and functions where substitution is either impossible or dysfunctional. We are all necessary, and this is what must be affirmed. Men and women are necessary before saying anything else, whether we are complementary or supplementary.

Each one of us is, and we must perceive ourselves as a complete good, ready to add up. That is our necessary contribution to society. A contribution that is given through the diversity of tasks, functions, capacities, relationships, and conditioned modes of dependence assumed in freedom. The line that one has been following, for some time now, when explaining gender, is a line that affirms it. It exists, from the social point of view, and we believe that the discipline that can most properly study it is sociology.

One has never had a problem with grammatical gender. Many years ago, at school, when they talked about grammatical genders, I was told that the grammatical genders were masculine, feminine, neuter, common, epicene, and ambiguous, and thanks to that classification and typology, the one that came later, between masculine, feminine, and neuter words, I have seen as a reductionism that would cause problems, as indeed it has happened. People do not understand words of common, epicene, and ambiguous gender, which there are as well as masculine, feminine, and neuter. The grammatical gender, then, does not concern me at all, and I am not in favor of changing the grammar to adapt an ideological gender discourse to the preferences of each one.

Beyond language, by saying that gender exists and that it is different from sex, we are referring to values. This implies, therefore, that gender can be changed. Oh, what nonsense you have just said! I have not said any nonsense, gender *can* be changed, and I will try to explain. Sex is fixed by biological and genetic markers that we have in each of the cells of our body. It is assigned to us before we are born. But gender, insofar as it is valuational, has a cultural dimension that can be changed historically in processes of long duration that can exceed the span of a lifetime. Hence, if gender is values, gender does not apply only to individuals, it does not apply only to people, it also applies to institutions and groups. Thus, regardless of its composition, the army has a masculine gender and the church, in the words of Pope Francis, a feminine one.

We are referring to constitutive values, which, although they can change through the course of history, it is more difficult in institutions than in people. It is true that, regardless of gender, one can identify in his or her way of acting, operating, understanding, or comprehending with more feminine values or with more masculine values. But what are masculine and feminine values? Well, they are those that history and cultural development or evolution propose to us as such, assigning roles, expectations, appearances, smells, virtues, defects, patterns, and manners. We can say that human history has proposed evolving generic value distinctions. Thus, for example, competitiveness, profit, initiative, autonomy, and the relegation of domestic duties in favor of work have generally been proposed to us as masculine values, while the spirit of understanding, service, complementarity, cooperation, interdependence, and domestic fulfillment have been proposed to us mostly as feminine values. The proposition is historically evolving, and we may be changing those values now. We may indeed change them over time, but we may not. This means that to the extent that one chooses one or the other, one can change gender. And I am speaking or writing to you from someone who considers herself to be of the female gender, or someone who thinks that today it is more important to emphasize feminine values than masculine ones.

That this is difficult to understand, well, maybe it is (this is my experience as a teacher), but one does not understand that the difficulty is so great that it reaches the point of rejection. It must be because one believes that the approaches advocated by the misnamed gender ideology and many so-called feminist proposals today are, from a value point of view, more sexist than anything else. Moreover, I think that machismo is what dominates the relationship between the sexes today. The objection that may come to the fore, at any moment, is that I am now saying that sex and gender have nothing to do with each other. From the institutional and collective point of view it is clear that they do not, but from the point of view of individuals they do have something to do with each other. They are related in the sense that through the psyche and education sex influences gender, but not the other way around. In any case, it is necessary to maintain the distinction in order not to think, as many people do, that if I can change gender, if I can change values, sex can also be changed. That is, as I understand it, impossible.

There are two somewhat biographical issues that I would like to bring up in this regard because I think they can shed some light on the discourse that we are following so far. One has to do with my childhood. As a child I was an inveterate reader; in fact, when I was very young, before my first communion, my mother always scolded me, telling me that I was going to lose my eyesight from reading so much. I liked to read about history and Greek tragedies, and as soon as I had the use of reason, I looked at the so-called history of Spain (I prefer history "in" Spain rather than history "of" Spain). I realized that in all the generations that had preceded me, throughout all the years of that history, the boys had to go to war. And then, when I realized that I was a man, I had no choice but to tell myself, "You will have to go to war," which was a big trauma for me, because I didn't see the point then (and I don't see the point now). One year, the Three Wise Men brought me a toy gun as a Christmas present, and then the thought that I had to go to war was confirmed, so I told myself that I would most probably have to kill somebody in my lifetime. No one could save me, I told myself, traumatized, from the obligation to kill someone if I wanted to survive. What a horrible conclusion! Thank goodness it hasn't happened, at least in my generation, and the war toys are being phased out.

The other experience took place in Kenya, where I was on a research stay at a United Nations agency. I got to know the country and was positively affected by the so-called African disease—the desire to return and come back to Africa once you have been there. I was also struck by the prostration of men in nearby villages and in Nairobi itself. During fieldwork, I asked why men are seen lying in the streets drunk, surrounded by misery, with nothing to do (looking at the statistics, I also knew the low life expectancy of men), while women were not seen in that deplorable state. One of the people accompanying me told me that there had been a break in the division of labor. The country had not yet assimilated the suppression of the old classic division of labor, in which the men devoted themselves either to hunting or to war and the women devoted themselves to the house and the fields, so when hunting and war disappeared, the men found themselves with nothing to do.

There is a long way to go, both in the relationship between the sexes and in the understanding of gender. We do not want to raise here any kind of pugnacity or competition (a macho value), nor any novel proposal of a political nature around gender, but we would like to see the virulence that is currently present in the debate diminish. It does not seem very academic to us that even mentioning the issue of gender ideology constitutes a casus belli. Rather, I believe that what should be done would be to elaborate proposals for cooperation and understanding that, in view of the social problems we face, would affirm the spirit of service over competitiveness. That, for a start, would be enough.

As far as the limit in general is concerned, the proposal we make is along the lines of emphasizing humility. We are limited, something that comes from our condition as creatures. But at the same time, we can realize it, something that derives from our rational capacity. In this regard, if someone said that humility is to be in the truth, I think he was right.

7. The Home

WE PRESENT HERE THE home as a terminal station, as opposed to two other ideal types of home, that of the home-fortress and that of the home-commune. The home is the exclusive sphere of the family, which gives it its most precise significance.

Some time ago I read a book by Byung-Chul Han, the previously mentioned German-Korean thinker, in which he distinguished thing from non-thing. Well, we are going to try to distinguish between home and non-home, starting from a definition that we are going to give from the beginning, without prejudice to others that we will give later. The home is the exclusive space of the family and, as such, both the space where family relations are cemented from the inside and strangeness, the distinction from the outside, is also cemented. Perhaps we should begin with a bit of self-criticism. It could be said that the social sciences, in general, have devoted little attention to the private sphere, to the home, for example, and have almost always focused their reflections on the public sphere. This has been a mistake, because where we humans spend most time is in private life—specifically, in the home. Humans confine the limits of our intimacy to the home, and the home is the shelter of the first community. For this reason, the home is an important and capital point of reflection for the social sciences.

It is not surprising, looking at history, that when people began to vote in political elections, the so-called heads of households had the right to vote. This transition from the *domus* to the *polis* was made considering households as political subjects. How interesting it would be, we think, without resorting again to that "one household one vote" but to one person one vote, if the *domus*, the households, would also be the center of political reflection today. In the social sciences, perhaps the scholar of reference for reflecting on the household is the aforementioned Norbert Elias, particularly a book he wrote in 1939, *The Civilizing Process*. There he echoes various contributions, from those of Freud in *Culture and Its Discontents* (1930) to the

Renaissance writings of Erasmus of Rotterdam and Luis Vives of Valencia. The former wrote *De civilitate* (1530) and the latter wrote the *Introducción a la Sabiduría* (1524) and *La Educación de las Mujeres* (1528). In both authors as well as in Freud, civilization is understood as a process that starts at home, is born in private life, and goes to public life. This is how Elias also understands it in his magnum opus, *The Civilizing Process*, where he says that civilization is neither more nor less than that which in many countries, for a long time now, has been called urbanity. Civilization means repression, self-control in behavior, and this control is first exercised at home, learned at home, and, by extension, later manifested in the public sphere.

We must also refer to Émile Durkheim, who, in his first great work, for the completion of his doctoral thesis, "On the Division of Social Labor" (1893), speaks of the necessary division of labor so that society can function organically. This applies to both the public and private spheres. The household begins to be defined, then, as a unit of production and consumption, as an environment where intangible goods are produced, where a unit of coexistence is formed on the basis of kinship ties, and where common consumption takes place. In this sense, the home is an emotionally charged space that protects intimacy and configures status or, at least, insertion into one. This was also pointed out by one of the first American sociologists, Thorstein Veblen, in a book called *The Theory of the Leisure Class* (1899). But first we are going to bring up Max Weber and the methodology of ideal types, which we believe will help us greatly in thinking about the household.

Referring to our time, to today and now, the ideal types applied to the home would be those environments and spaces of identity relations that we might refer to as the cosmovisions of the *domus*, the *polis*, and the cosmos itself. From the point of view of the cosmos, the ideal type that would propose the figure of the home is the fortress home. The fortress home is that alternative universe protected by high walls in which one lives differently from how one lives outside. The fortress home has a defensive wall and is separated from the rest of society.

From the point of view of the *polis*, the ideal type that we could design is the republic household or the commune household where the symbiotic society there somehow reseeds the *polis*. If we were to translate this into political terms, the worldview or ideal type of the fortress home would be on the right, while the worldview or ideal type of the republic or commune home would be on the left.

It is also worth tracing the ideal type that we are going to place in the center, which is the terminal station home. The terminal station home is like an initiatory journey. There are arrivals and departures, and one leaves with baggage, with beliefs, and with nostalgia.

These three types of ideals are present in literature; they intermingle and are also proposed. We would like to propose the one we have placed in the center, the terminal station home. The fortress home has advantages as well as many disadvantages. It is an overprotective home. It marks the differences between home and non-home, and it marks them so much that in a way it makes the home the antithesis of society. There is a very large containment pit between the public and the private. In the communal home the opposite situation occurs. There is very little separation between the public sphere and the private sphere to the point that they can be identified, blurring the private sphere because the public sphere is much stronger. Here, the strangeness that protects the family is no longer perceived as necessary. The hierarchy between parents or progenitors and children as well as the distinction between nuclear family and extended family disappears. The republic or commune home blurs the family home. On the contrary, the terminal station home not only welcomes new members into our society but also prepares them for the journey: it equips them, gives them a culture, values, and an understanding of life in society, which enables them to form, later on, other similar homes. Thus, the diachrony that is lived within the family, which is the relationship between parents, children, grandchildren, etc., the succession of generations, would also be lived harmoniously outside the family, in society, in that train that leaves the terminal station perfectly equipped and prepared to reach hidden places.

There is, in the terminal station home, a relevance of things because the terminal station differs from the passing station in that it is much better equipped. The family that equips its home takes into account the importance of the material instruments—for example, the furniture. A space inhabited by things that in some way dignify themselves by becoming a reference point because they challenge us and underpin our identity. How many times have we felt identified, among siblings, with a piece of furniture or with something material that was in our parents' house, when our parents' house was our house.

This idea of materialization is linked to furniture and, in some contexts, even a flashy or luxurious piece of furniture. This should not be forgotten as our digital world is forgetting about things, something Han points out (in the book mentioned above) about the distinction between thing and nonthing. The relevance of the material will again give importance to things as in the terminal stations, which can compete to see which one is the best, the coziest, or the one with the best services. And if we try to point out which is the most important element, I would dare to say that it is the key. The key to the fortress home is immense; it is a very heavy key that opens enormous, tremendously heavy doors. The key does not exist in the republic or commune home, but in the terminal station home the key exists in its proper mobile capacity. Without a key there is no distinction between home and non-home. How important it would be that in our homes we rethink the role of the key. Who has it, who does not have it, who uses it, who can use it, and at what times.

We must also think that the home is the environment that justifies inequality. Nowadays, there is a lot of talk about equality, which, in terms of equality before the law, makes perfect sense. But we do not talk so much about the inequality that makes us who we are when we are different. It is an inequality that goes from the home outwards, that sows and cares for the personality of each one of us, that dresses us as humans who have names and surnames, but also domiciles, a spatial anchorage that is also relational. This inequality gives plurality to the environment and, therefore, brings richness to society. Homes should provide and welcome diversity so we can calibrate the scales. Not all terminal stations are the same. There are better and worse, but in any case, we should try that our terminal station home provides an environment that calls for affection. Some say that the family is the place to which one returns. Well, a terminal station is always welcoming to the arriving train. To make a home is to turn cold transit stations into welcoming terminal stations.

There are those who think that a family without a home is possible. I believe it is not. There are also those who postulate virtual homes. And this author believes that this confuses home with non-home. It is here where we understand the importance we give to the unfortunate and pernicious increase of homeless people today, because the disappearance in quality and quantity of homes is a symptom of barbarism. The process of civilization, which is linked to civility, to the importance of manners, of knowing how to behave, and to the transfer of that wisdom of everyday life, which makes up humanity, goes through the home. Civilization comes to us in the home, and then it is carried out in the public spheres. We become socially competent to the extent that we trust others. It is absurd that we all try to do everything; we become unhinged. The division of labor gives shape to the social ties that are born in the home as a tiny organic society.

Rematerialization here is not materialism. It is giving new value to material things in the face of the digital invasion. Digitalization, in a way, unifies us all on a large scale, and the home has to be, in the face of digitalization, a disuniformizing element, a retaining wall against unwanted invasions. We cannot be children of the network, we are children of our parents, because, as we will see later, and we will not fail to point out, filiation is the radical character of the human.

8. Care

WE ELABORATE HERE A critique of the educational system and a proposal of replacement that assumes the family protagonism and the importance of the care and promotion of the capacities. A pedagogical approach that may seem groundbreaking and, at the same time, in our opinion, necessary.

It may seem strange that an advocate of homeschooling and a fierce critic of the government's efforts to arrogate to itself the exclusive right to educate now jumps into the limelight to say something about the educational system. I think that the subjection of education to the constituted powers perpetuates and consolidates a command that is exercised with impunity over children and young people. It has a certain totalitarian and fascistic whiff. These powers impose plans, programs, and content while turning a deaf ear to internal criticism and persecuting dissidence. This is combined with denunciations against the imaginary defects, which they say are detected in those who do not bend or do things differently.

In almost all countries there is talk today of the failure of education, of the immaturity of youth, and of the flight of governmental educational monopolies from the reality of the world and its needs. The fact is, when you think about it a little more seriously, all education has a lot of manipulation, as all history has a lot of fiction, and as all training in regulatory regimentation has a lot of imposition. I could be asked: are you saying, then, that we should close all schools and give up the transmission of knowledge? Not exactly, but I am saying that we must rethink the educational system from top to bottom, rethinking education as care.

For this purpose, I believe that we should begin our reflection long before the recurrent debate on training or information. I am of the opinion that the primordial care and mental protection that children and young people need in today's world lies in what the ancients called self-mastery. To master oneself or to be mastered, this is the dilemma facing the future of our children, whether they go to school or not, and we must try as a society and as parents to ensure that the scales are tipped on the side of self-mastery. But I was saying that we have to position ourselves a little before this, before even considering, if it should come to that, which I doubt, the transmission of any standardized and obligatory informative content for all.

It was Amartya Sen and, later in another sense, Amitai Etzioni who made me reflect and go deeper into all this. The human being, more than an animal, is, for the subject that concerns us, like a plant. A plant that, taking for granted its constitutive reality, that is to say, what is implied by a soil where it settles, which we understand to be akin to the germ of virtues, a climate in which it lives healthily, which are the values it carries, and a differentiated seed, which are its innate potentialities, which we will call here capacities, must be cared for, and a lot, so that it can bear fruit. This care will then have three main tasks, and, as in the plant world, we will talk about irrigation, fertilizer, and pest control.

But that will come later. Now it is pertinent to say, with regard to education, we have talked a lot about virtues and values but not so much about capacities. That is why I wanted to bring all this into account. Values are loves, virtues are habits, capacities are potencies. In my opinion, if there is one value that we must try to discover as early as possible in our loved ones, it is the love of freedom. If there is a habit that we must give to our children in the first place, it is the habit of order, to differentiate the goals and regulate the achievable steps to reach them. But what about capabilities? Of them, little or almost nothing is spoken. They are, in our opinion, as important as the values and the virtues. If we want to take good care, it is necessary to enhance the capabilities of each person from early childhood.

As is the case with virtues and values, a wide and varied list of human capabilities can be drawn up. I like to stick mainly to four of them: will, skills, sensitivity, and imagination. Will is not a force, and the expression "willpower" does not seem to me to be entirely appropriate. Rather, it is a compound of sense, wisdom, and constancy. Sense, in the first place, is to aim at the required objective, which basically involves distinguishing the good from the passions and setting one's sights on discernible goods that are purposeful and affable, i.e., dear. In the second place, wisdom to verify the proposal and have the capacity to rectify without the motivation clouding the consequences of the action to avoid the so-called voluntarism. And thirdly, constancy, to assimilate the passage of time by persevering in our work and to be able to grow inside at the same time as we grow outside.

Skills, on the other hand, are both physical and mental abilities that require exercise to make them personally useful. Among them, and given the situation of neglect and rejection that educational systems attribute to effort, merit, and excellence, it seems important to me to incorporate as goals

of care, firstly, self-respect: an urbanity of knowledge that, through a balance between shame and confidence, gives wings to intuition and initiative;
secondly, memory, on which much of the cultural background depends; and
thirdly, analysis, which forms the backbone of criticism.

Sensitivity is, on the other hand, the appreciation of materialized and
embodied values that enable both the enjoyment of beauty and the exercise of understanding. Sensitivity, as a capacity, is educable as a response of
interpellation. Not only to value or admire the beautiful but, more importantly, to calibrate the response we give to beauty and to recognize the way
in which beauty humanizes and unites us.

Finally, imagination, which we will focus on immediately, as we believe
it is in serious crisis. A pedagogy based fundamentally on capabilities has
yet to be discovered and built. The educational system has been criticized
for the absence of values and virtues and, as usual, very little has been done
about it. It has not been questioned, however, about the decline of capabilities because, as we say, little or nothing is said about it. While recalling its
importance, we would like to make a spearhead here on the need to care for
the imagination, which is the capacity on which we are going to focus our
attention. Caring for the imagination, in the sense of helping it to grow, is
one of the most important tasks in accompanying a child or young person
toward maturity.

If capacities are, in general, undervalued by the educational system,
imagination is often scorned with disdain. We do not realize how indispensable it is to understand, comprehend, and improve reality. Undertaking
something, anything, from a life project to a professional initiative, begins
with seeing or imagining a deficiency that can be fixed. That is why it is
so important to imagine well. We cannot imagine backward, molding the
past (although many try to do so), but we can aspire to see the reality that
is going to be and is not yet, imagining it correctly from the evidence of the
present.

The reality that is to be is not pure fiction but, properly speaking, divine providence. It is certainly unknowable but real and, as such, existent.
In this sense, imagination is the realism of idealism, while mere fiction is
its failure. Therefore, imagination does not distance us from reality but
rather illuminates it, endowing it with verisimilitude insofar as that reality
has been well perceived. On the contrary, fiction as a deceitful imagination,
when it is not understood as a lie or a playful assumption, can prevent us
from recognizing the reality in which we live and are. How important it is,
then, not only to imagine but, above all, to imagine well.

It will be necessary to remember which are the most important tools
and obstacles to take care of to protect the development of imagination in

our children. In our opinion, the main tool is the narrative story, the fairy tale, the illustrated conversation, and, above all, reading. This is, as we said, the watering of the plant. On the other hand, the most important obstacle is deception. Herein lies the plague. That is why we believe that to deceive a child is to deprive them of the confidence necessary to recognize reality as it is. It is a sin against humanity that we must never compromise in exchange for anything in the world. The fertilizer of imaginations, on the other hand, is the security provided by the environment and, fundamentally, by the family, which is where one should read. The family that neither reads nor converses bogs down, restricts, and nullifies the imagination of its youngsters. This leads us to a pertinent and continuous reflection that everyone should make on family time, which we could conceive as being with. To accompany, to be in, to take care of, and to be without being bored seems to us to be a very necessary occupation, which we simply leave noted so as not to go off on a tangent.

I am not, as you may have already seen, at all optimistic about the changes that may take place in the educational system regarding the importance of taking care of skills as well as virtues and values. And I am even less optimistic about the possible positive effects that screens and other technological gadgets that encourage pernicious addictions can have on the care of the imagination. In the alliance between school, which embodies and proposes the current educational system, and technology, we see an oppressive axis that exerts an omnipotent force precisely on those with less power: our children. Hence the current formal and informal educational system is, in our opinion, a petty disaster and an exercise in manipulation on a scale never seen before, which, moreover, prioritizes the annulment of the best by cutting off the possibilities of self-mastery as one of its main latent objectives.

But for all these reasons, we are optimistic about the positive results that the negation of this system, starting with the commitment to an optional school and the suppression of compulsory education, can have for our young people. To truly care for them in freedom, focusing on the growth and transformation that their powers, habits, and loves can bring about in themselves and in us at the same time. Undoubtedly, to get there, we must begin by applying the recipe to our own flesh.

We must be imaginative. If we are up to the task, why not send the current educational system and the state as an educating agent to the back room of overcome nightmares while we each assume our possible caring responsibilities toward our children? I do not believe in the goodness of the ministries of education, nor of their study plans; rather, I am a supporter of educational freedom, of the option of education in the family, of the guarantor state being responsible for minimum surveillance so that at a certain age each child knows how to communicate properly, which are the current rules of public coexistence. I am also in favor of the public administration closest to the people providing the necessary educational infrastructures free of charge, so they can be used by the families who wish to do so, in the way they wish, under regimes of service and plural use. But it does not seem convenient to me at all to confuse care with imposition, nor to grant to any government any type of monopoly on the moral education that should be imparted by the educational agents, us, as caretakers of our children, or whoever we designate.

9. The Family

LET US NOW FOCUS, as announced, on the family. We will focus on the sovereign family as a counterweight to state power. We will advocate for more familiar and less state environments, where this sovereignty with personality, distinction, liturgy, and own norms can be concretized.

We begin by referring to a surprising issue for anyone who has written on the sociology of the family. In fact, many of the themes that we are going to discuss below are dealt with in a book that is already some years old but which we believe is still valid, *Rethinking the Family* (2015). That topic was the intervention of St. John Paul II in *Gratissimam Sane* (1994), when he spoke of the sovereignty of the family. Thus, these two characteristics of this writer—that of a sociologist who is, more or less, an expert in the family, and that of a Christian—make this reference of the holy pope to the sovereignty of the family produce a more than pleasant surprise, which we have not ceased to think about over the years.

We have chosen four themes or cardinal points that can illuminate what family sovereignty means and how it can help us to understand the family, understand society, and understand the future of the world as well as how it can be a program that helps us to live better. Those four points are: personality, distinction or strangement, liturgy, and norms and routines. Let's go point by point.

When we speak of *personality*, we refer to the subject. The family, which has personality because it is sovereign, must be understood as a subject—something that is by no means common. We speak of a subject of rights but also of an economic subject, a political subject, and a civil subject. If we think of the family as a subject of rights, we will have to articulate some rights of the family. If we think of the family as an economic subject, we will consider not only the expenses incurred by the family but also its income. We will take into consideration, for example, whether it is time to talk about a family salary or whether this family salary should be reflected in individual salaries, something that would change, one believes positively, the whole economy. When we speak of the family as a civil subject, we are insisting that divorce should be rethought. The way in which divorce is applied today, without taking into consideration the family nucleus—particularly the victims of its disappearance, who are the children, specifically the minors—goes against the condition of family subject that we are giving to the family. Divorce certainly needs to be rethought; it should not be taken for granted in all cases. The consideration, we see, of the family as a subject of the family personality is something that has a long reach.

If we move on to the second point, distinction, we mean that families can be distinguished from one another. This is what we have called *strangeness*. Strangeness has to do with the other, and the other cannot be imposed on us in the sense that we should not understand the other in a univocal way. The other in the family is the stranger, not the self. Strangers exist because our own exist, that is why families are distinguishable. My own are different from your own, dear reader, and it is here that no one, not even the state, can impose any other on me as my own. My strangers are also distinct from their strangers. The other is properly seen and calibrated from the familiar consideration. The radicality that separates own and strangers is the radicality that configures the other, and it is a radicality that configures a different other always. Thus, the fact that the others for the own are never the same humanizes the other, who, if he is another, who, if he is strange to me, can be his own for many other families.

The distinction that strangeness procures can be argued in many ways distant from the family nucleus, but there is the progeny, there is the family name, and there are the traditions proper to the family that procure a peculiar relationship to a great number of people. For that reason, the distinction, the strangeness, adds plurality to a society. It is not the state that should impose the other on me, impose on me in the sense of pointing him out or pointing out to me who my strangers are, no. It is the family that tells me who my strangers are, who the other is. An other who must also be protected without ceasing to be other.

Let us go now to the *liturgy*, which we understand as the basic customs that make the family's own functions operative. Each family carries out these operations, which we call functions, in different ways. This is really where it all lies. In the four functions of the family, there is everything or almost everything that can and should be said about the family. I have studied and reflected on these functions in several of my works, and they are: *cultural transmission*, *social control*, *socialization*, and *generational equity*. Here, we can add that how to perform these functions is the basis of freedom. It is the freedom of the family, which must be allowed to implement these functions, and it is freedom from the family, because to the extent that one benefits in his family, from these functions well carried out, one will become effectively free. In the liturgy of the family, in how these customs are articulated, which we have called functions to the extent that they are necessary and that constitute in some way the family nucleus, we also make a somewhat veiled allusion to diachrony. Generational equity is precisely that: how a family takes care of its elders as well as its minors. Hence, the liturgies themselves characterize the family unit in a dissimilar way.

Finally, we speak, fourthly, of *norms and routines*. We refer to norms *ab intra*, that is, the family's daily activities, and to norms *ab extra*, that is, the social responsibility of the family toward the outside world. As far as the former are concerned, there is that binomial that must always be mentioned when speaking of the family, which is the one between authority and family diversity. Not all families articulate their internal authority in the same way; rather, they do so in a diverse manner, mediated by family traditions manifested around two key moments: the feast and the mourning. They are a manifestation of verticality: the *ab intra* norms articulate the family verticality, something that has to do with diachrony, around the cultural heritage articulated in experiences. There are ways of doing, of commanding, or of obeying.

If we refer to the *ab extra* norms, we count on the fact that social responsibility is fundamentally manifested in welcoming. We point out the other because the other often needs to be welcomed without ceasing to be other. The social responsibility of the family necessarily implies civil participation or religious participation, and here, in the same way that in the norms inside we have referred to verticality, horizontality applies.

These four notes of family sovereignty have great repercussions and trajectory. Personality, distinction, liturgy, and norms, to the extent that they are well understood, will help to understand and value the concept of sovereign family. The sovereign family refers to power, or rather, it refers to independence from power. It is an application of subsidiarity. When we raise this slogan of more family and less state, we are referring to subsidiarity, that the state stops making the family, that it does not supplant it, and that, at the same time, the state acts when the family does not operate. That only when the family does not arrive, then the state arrives, because as long as the family arrives, as long as this happens, there will be more humanity, more justice, and, above all, more freedom.

Understanding the family as a responsible subject gives plurality to society, gives freedom, and takes power away from the state, but, at the same time, sustains and bases the responsibility of the individuals who live in the family unit. We must understand the sovereign family as something dynamic. The family lives in time, in a time that is age and in a time that is culture, and in the same way that one, when one has years, occupies a place in the family and when one has other years occupies another place. In some way, this changes many things within the family. Also, when time passes, culturally speaking, families can configure their patterns in a different way. We humans are cultural beings. Families adapt and must conform to the culture of their time. This is why the study of the family is fundamental to sociology and has many implications for the history of culture. The study of the family also proposes some of the most important goals for economics or for the judicial harmonization of a more equitable and just society. The study of the family will illuminate those gaps of freedom that need to be filled. For all these reasons, it is only fair to thank St. John Paul II for speaking, in his day, of family sovereignty.

We would be leaving the subject of sovereignty lame if we did not mention two other issues before addressing positive inequality as a corollary to our argument. One is the opportunity to refer to a debate very present in today's culture about the end of modernity and its impact on the family, contrasting dependence and autonomy. The other is that the family puts freedom in its place insofar as it imposes a process of dynamic discovery of each person's capacity for self-possession. Here the relevance of containment underlines the need to create an account of one's own memory on the road to self-mastery.

When dealing with the family and autonomy, it will be necessary to go slowly, as we have already shown in the book *Pasar el testigo* (2020), or *Passing the Baton*, in which we dealt with the family reality from the point of view of diachrony. Regarding autonomy, many believed that it was one of the modern panaceas. But no, autonomy is an illusion, not to say a delusion. Autonomy affirms or promises things that it cannot give, because when we contemplate ourselves from what we really are, and we are familiar beings, we observe the primacy of dependency relationships. In making this reflection, the point is to break down how dependency is articulated and that we should not lament the fact that this lowers the spirits of autonomy. On the contrary, one thinks, we should celebrate it, because digging deeper and discovering our dependencies, in the end, puts each of us in front of the mirror.

Someone might think that we should be very careful if we are going to criticize autonomy, because we might be doing away with freedom. Not at all; quite the contrary. In fact, let us look at some of the negative understandings of freedom. One thinks that the first and foremost exercise of freedom is its voluntary renunciation. Understand me well, what we discover with dependence is that what I can do is not the same as what I must do, and it is not good, it is not an exercise of freedom, to do all that I can do.

Righteousness in the renunciation of evil is a predicate of freedom. Freedom is, we understand, self-possession, and in that self-possession, we discover our duties while rejecting the dominion of others. Freedom that does not reject the dominion of others, but rather seeks it, is not freedom but slavery.

The family is genuinely a school of freedom. Unfortunately, this has not been seen to be the case, mostly among our colleagues in the discipline. There are many sociologists who, rather than discovering the family from which each of us comes insofar as we are radically daughters and sons, rather than discovering this verticality in the social, by focusing exclusively on the horizontal, have gone with egoism. Egoism is antisocial, self-referential, and puts profit and self-interest on a pedestal. Consequently, egoism leads us to relativism. The family is there, among other things, to save us from this, because we are not "I" before being a daughter or a son, we are not individuals before being social; society, specifically the family, precedes us and will follow us. This does not go against freedom. These dependencies discover us, and one is only free when one discovers oneself.

But let us see what it means to say that the family is a school of freedom. Here, in the family, we become aware of our internal dependencies as, at the same time, we become aware of our external independences. It is in this opposition between family and established powers that we discover ourselves capable of being free. It is not hidden from us that the established powers, as we manifest in *Sobrepoder* (2005), have never been so great, neither in quantity nor in quality, thanks to or because of globalization and technology—to the point that these established powers have created new colonialisms. We speak, for example, of ludic colonialisms related to gambling, in which one participates with money throughout the world twenty-four hours a day, or of colonialisms that have to do with art, particularly with fashion, to the point that fashion itself has an effect on how we present ourselves anywhere on the planet. The established powers have exerted a tremendous influence to the point of often hiding the family, transforming sane dependencies into evil addictions and plurality into uniformity.

There was a belief in the linear development of progress, and we were supposed to be doomed to progress. This gave us such a security, such a tremendous self-confidence, that we thought that the family was like an ornament. No, it is not like that. Throughout our transit in it, we passed from a radical dependence to discover ourselves and, therefore, to think that we are capable of being free. Only he who knows himself, who discovers himself, who knows who he is, can aspire to be free. The family creates binding dependencies, and at the same time, in these dependencies, it creates us. I will never cease to be the child of who I am, whether I want it or not. It is an innate and radical dependence.

We discover here a contraposition between the so-called modern powers and the powers of the future, which will be able to enable us for self-possession to the extent that we discover ourselves as familiar beings. It is in this contraposition that the concept of freedom dances. We are free when at the same time we are self-possessed and when we renounce the possession of others. The two things go together and the result is self-mastery: to dominate ourselves. This is why we have spoken of a negative conception of freedom: knowing how to say no to ourselves.

Apart from the family being a school of freedom, the family is also a school of friendship. It is important to underline this because friends are free and, at the same time, mutually dependent. There is here a kind of contrast between a negative pole that we call abandonment and a positive pole that we call commitment. Abandonment for the sake of the autonomy of a binding duty is a failure for the one who abandons as well as a failure for the whole society. Commitment, on the other hand, underlines the choice of duty and is, unlike abandonment, a personal and social success. If I abandon my parents, if I abandon my children, I harm them, perhaps irreparably. On the contrary, if I do not abandon or neglect them but protect them, I serve them. For therein lies the difference between what sustains a healthy society and what leads a society to collective failure.

The family, by making it possible for us to distinguish autonomy as negative from self-mastery as positive, shows us that we need the freedoms of others, that we need the duties freely assumed by others, discovered by others, and that it is these duties that will save us and take care of us when we become patients. In this sense, we depend, conceptually speaking, more on the family than on the state, and it will be a good thing if this is indeed the case, also in that future we will hopefully reach, when this change of epoch between the already imperilled modernity and what comes after it is really consolidated.

It is not strange that some thinkers, such as the French Fabrice Hadjahj, advocate a substitution in which he advocates more religion, of *religare*, of a bond of dependence, and less state, of omnipotent power. It is in the family that we find a guarantee of freedom. The state offered us the illusion of autonomy. Our peculiar identities are the binding dependencies that, in each one of us, are different. Some dependencies are innate, in the case of the family, for example, and other dependencies are acquired, which is the history of our choices and affinities. No, unbounded autonomy was a deception; autonomy, moreover, is not something precious—autonomy leaves us alone, it isolates us. What a surprise, and we come back to it, that some of our colleagues agree in advocating this isolation, which is like a dereliction of the duty we have not only to do sociology, but to demonstrate its necessity.

There are two more authors I wanted to mention before I finish these two points and move on to inequality. One is Dwight MacDonald, who, when he was very young, wrote a wonderful book called *The Root Is Man* (1946), a text that has been widely published. MacDonald advocates the concept of the limit of contention. He says that the negativity of containment is a consequence of the positivity of freedom, and that it is very healthy to speak of the limits of freedom. Here, we reaffirm that beyond responsibility, there is no freedom. The other author is Alasdair McIntyre, who in a tremendously suggestive book entitled *Dependent Rational Animals* breaks a lance in favor of sociology and affirms that all rational inquiry is a social inquiry. He defends the social character of the virtues (his favorite theme). Virtues, he says, form bonds, bonds of relationship and friendship, and through these relationships we discover our particularity.

How important the social is. We go to the individual, from the collective we go to the personal; it is not the other way around. Autonomy is not the first thing. Unbounded autonomy, as we have already said, is an illusion because we are more dependent than autonomous. Dependencies which, whether we like it or not, are there and which we recognize when we study the family. It is not strange that we say that the family is yet to be discovered. It is not only to be discovered in the sense of valuing each one of us, but it is also to be discovered in the academic field, in research. It is yet to be discovered because it is also yet to be proposed.

How is it possible, we ask ourselves, that in politics and economics the family is not yet considered a sovereign subject, that both politics and economics consider the autonomous individual as the preferred subject? It is not true, and it is necessary that in both cases, in politics and economics, the family be integrated. In some of my texts I have proposed ways of integration by talking about the vote of children and other initiatives. There are many ways, but mainly we should open our minds to the family being present in the political discourse, in the economic discourse, not only as an object, not only as something that consumes, but as something that produces essential and irreplaceable immaterial goods.

But let us enter fully into a last matter to be considered, which is that the family is the proper sphere of inequality. There are fair and proper inequalities and unfair and improper inequalities. Studying them from a family perspective implies talking about deficiencies, immaterial poverty, and positive poverty, concepts that are very useful to see which inequalities are incompatible with justice and which equalities are incompatible with freedom.

I have sometimes heard the expression that, since the family and equality are incompatible, the family will have to be replaced. I might have heard this other expression, that, as family and equality are incompatible, equality should be dispensed with. But this second expression, I have neither heard nor read it yet. It is not, in any case, the pertinent question. The pertinent question, it seems to me, is which equalities and inequalities are incompatible with freedom and justice. And this question, when asked from the point of view of the family, has a reading, more or less, as follows: starting from the fact that the family is something constitutive of what is human, what must be asked is which equalities and which inequalities are incompatible with it. Being, let us remember, because we have always been told this, comes before doing; life comes before law.

All well and good, but in line with what we are saying, there is an issue that emerges as a priority, and it is that of measurement: how we measure inequalities and how we measure equality. In sociology, this measurement has been done somewhat in the wake of the enthusiasm of economists, looking at or following the optics of the study of poverty. Thus, inequality has been measured by measuring income. That is a mistake because poverty is something very complex. When talking about poverty, we should not only look at material poverty. I prefer to talk more about inequality than equality and more about deprivation than poverty. In any case, when it comes to understanding what poverty is, it would be good to make a prior distinction between material poverty and immaterial poverty.

Some people may be surprised by the term immaterial poverty, which is associated with immaterial deprivation. Deprivations that may be related to identity, to freedom, but which are also related to other aspects of life, such as affective poverty, relational poverty, participatory poverty, environmental poverty, or political-expressive poverty. And then, everything that derives from lack of security, pluralism, freedoms, such as lack of religious freedom, lack of freedom of opinion, etc. Immaterial poverty is more a poverty of ends than of means, and Amartya Sen has given us important lessons on this, telling us that immaterial collective goods, in the long run, eradicate material needs.

There is a relationship between immaterial poverty and material poverty, but we can also say that there are immaterial evils that produce unjust inequalities. One looks at the desire to dominate, at over-power, but there is also an immaterial poverty that has to do with material evils. Let us think, for example, of suicide, which is so much talked about today (and to which we will return later), of behavioral illnesses, of domestic violence, and of abuse. All these are material evils derived from immaterial poverty. This distinction between material poverty and immaterial poverty is very important when trying to measure deprivation and inequalities.

Another distinction that should be made when reflecting on the relationship between family and equality is the distinction between negative poverty and positive poverty. Positive poverty is a poverty sought and intended by those who aspire to be positively poor. We are talking about beneficial deficiencies, such as the lack of the aspiration to dominion, or that biunivocal substitution, which one has always recommended, in the sense that we would have a better world if we were able to substitute cooperation and the desire to serve for competitiveness and the desire for profit. There, cooperation and the spirit of service point to a positive poverty that is also the paradigm of the family economy. In the family there are positive poverties; there are deprivations for the benefit of those who most need the services of others. Hence, from the point of view of positive poverty, we could say that it is optimal to aspire to the maximization of detachment and the maximization of the gift, something that occurs fundamentally in the family.

Aspiring for one's personal worth to be measured in terms of positive poverty seems to us relevant and exemplifying. Personal worth is concretized in a threefold understanding of time: time generated (that which saves knowledge), time added (that which saves order), and time given (that which procures service). We humans are of value to the extent that we are of value to others when we give. We can apply this concept of positive poverty to institutions and corporations as well. It is certainly a difficult goal, particularly in some environments infected with neoliberal evils, to talk about it being a good aspiration to propose positive poverty in corporations. However, I believe that there should be such a positive goal in policy makers as well as entrepreneurs, so they can live a virtuous poverty in their organizations, undertakings, and proposals for public action.

There are some authors to whom, in this connection, I would like to pay tribute. One of them is an old acquaintance, because he was very enlightening at the time when I was more involved in research—the previously mentioned E. F. Schumacher and his book *Small Is Beautiful* (1973). He does not mention positive poverty in that book, but in reading the text one can draw the conclusion that there is a latent positive poverty to which we should all aspire. Another is the German-Korean Byung-Chul Han, also mentioned, who in *Buen Entretenimiento* (2018) and *La expulsion de lo distinto* (2017) speaks of the promotion of plurality in social life, something from which we can learn by contemplating the family in its horizontality, in fraternity. He also refers to the positive poverty that the lack of screens would imply. Two other authors are the Frenchman Pierre Rosanvallon, who wrote a book called *La Sociedad de los Iguales* (2012) in which he tells us that, please, in the name of equality, no more rights. And finally, an American author, Harry Frankfurt, who wrote *On Inequality* (2015), where he advises us not to look so much at the shortcomings of equality but at the concept of sufficiency.

These four authors are quite enlightening when it comes to relating the metaphor of the family as the family optimum to the issue of equality. We said that one prefers to speak of inequalities rather than equality because inequalities can be measured. When talking about inequalities, it would be good to consider, first, some necessary distinctions. There are inequalities that are, we could say, constitutive, such as genetic or biological inequalities or the fact that we do not all have the same life expectancy due to natural causes (understanding illness due to contingency as one of them). There are inequalities that apply, fundamentally, with the family, such as affective or patrimonial inequalities. And there are inequalities that depend on the place and time where and when one is born, on language, or on innate abilities. To aspire that all these inequalities do not exist in the world is crazy, even if there are people who aspire to it (transhumanists excuse themselves in that they pretend that these inequalities cease to be so). Let us also think that there are acquired inequalities that have to do with age, with property, with income, with the liberal choices one makes, with the use of freedom, with chance, or with merit. There is even an author who talks about cognitive inequalities, another about access to technology. Well, there are many criteria for measuring inequalities, and these criteria tell us that there are inequalities that it would be good to avoid as well as many others that it would be unfair to eliminate.

The perspectives we use to measure inequality vary greatly. There is a perspective that we could call economic-labor, and that is the one that most people look at, but there is also a legal perspective, since we are not all equal before the law, which admits exceptions, and it is good that it admits exceptions, such as the age of minority. There is the perspective of needs since we do not all have the same needs. We must not stigmatize inequality because difference is good and, more than that, it is good that we are different; indeed, it is better that each of us is unique. And here, again, we return to the family, because in the family we are unique. We propose the family as the paradigm on which the academy should focus to talk about equality, inequality, deprivation, and poverty.

Another relevant claim when measuring or trying to measure inequalities is the inequality of whom. We almost always look at individual subjects and their income, but what about collective subjects? It is hard to imagine that collective subjects, which have to do with identities, professions, or associations, should also be equal. This is certainly not the case. Among these collective subjects we can put the family. Thus, the family is the justified sphere of inequality. Let us never forget that. We have tried to make it clear that, indeed, deprivation is important, that immaterial poverty is important, and that positive poverty is important. In order to study inequality and equality, in order to evaluate the proposals that can be made on these issues, it is very good to look, first of all, at the family. To understand the family is to understand what we are.

10. Modernity

THE END OF OUR epochal cycle demands a precise reflection. We point out three interpretative assumptions of the new epoch that illuminate the end of modernity as well as the way to face its advent and what to try to save of the epoch that ends. Whether the transfer to the new is possible, fruitful, or critical depends on what we do now.

From the point of view of the modernity that is ending, everything is wrong. It is incorrect that modernity itself is ending, and it is incorrect that we speak of the end of one epoch and the beginning of another. But I do think it is good to point out the mistakes and obstacles that, even from the point of view of a modern critique, will first appear in this epoch that, thank God, is beginning to dawn. What I am going to say below I have outlined in two little works that I wrote, *Pequeña investigación sobre la caridad política* (2017) and an article, a little older, published in *Anales Valentinos Revista de Filosofía y Teología*, in which I gloss what I call "La cuarta cristiandad" or "The Fourth Christianity."

The framework in which we are operating, as has been said, is the end of modernity. A situation that has been denounced for many years now and that is concretized in the collapse of those assumptions on which a supposed era of progress and well-being that was supposed to last forever and that we call modernity had been built. These assumptions are, fundamentally, three: first, the change from the old to the new regime, which points to the birth of nationalism (nationalism, I believe, is one of the most perverse cancers in contemporary culture); second, rationality, or the preeminence of scientific-technical rationality, which points to the support of formalism over finalism (we are now realizing that formalism devoid of any purpose leads us to a meaningless bureaucratism, without a project and without a goal); and, thirdly, the conception of the idea of linear progress, a conception that since the first atomic bomb was dropped at the end of the Second World War has been put to rest by the atomic and environmental crises (of which we will speak later), which have brought down the idea of linear progress that had been in force until then. Modernity was built on these three great columns, now full of cracks and leading modernity to its finiteness. I was going to say its failure, but modernity has not failed, just as none of the previous epochs have failed, because we learn from everything and, at least so far, we have come out of everything.

I am going to refer to the incorrectness that, from the modern point of view, appears on the horizon. It will be good to detect and study because whatever comes after modernity positions itself in this respect. In my opinion, there are at least three of them. In the *first* place, there is the need to protect human identity, a need that becomes peremptory because the "development" of new biomedical techniques makes it necessary. The biological and neurological identity of individuals is threatened by transhumanism, biogenetic manipulation, and technological implants in the brain. In the face of this, it is necessary to affirm a humanistic anthropocentrism that will endow the culture that sustains whatever comes next with arguments that defend our biological and neurological identity. We cannot be subject to the continuous fear that any gadget that, without our consent or with our uninformed assent, is implanted and changes us, supposedly for the better or supposedly for the worse, to make us slaves or to make us live a time that none of us had thought to live. It is necessary that this era that is dawning is born with a certainty, from the biomedical point of view, that our identities are going to be preserved. That one will remain the same, and that no one will replace me, or that I will be someone other than who I am.

Secondly, there is the approach, which comes from the beginning of modernity, on the understanding of the demos, which is concretized in the perverse inheritance of individualism. Individualism, together with nationalism, in my opinion, are the two cancers that have been gradually gaining ground, eating away at the body of modernity. And to prevent this cancer of individualism from corrupting the new age that is now beginning to take shape, it is necessary to take precautions and measures. In my opinion, one of these measures is to rethink the subject and specifically to give a leading role to the family subject, as we have argued in the previous chapter. The family subject needs a representation in the public sphere that it does not have now, and in order for it to have it, we will have to rethink political representation in such a way as to include everyone, if representative democracy is still in force. It will be necessary to prevent structural inequalities from creeping in through the trap door of individualism, and, as has already been stated on other occasions, to this end, it will be advisable to rethink inheritance and succession, enlightening alternatives, which, at the same time, respect property and save equity. Some types of inheritance guarantee and consecrate an unjustified and avoidable level of inequality at the outset. It is true that the family has functions that point to inequalities that seem to us fair and necessary. But it does not seem to us so fair that these inequalities had to be imposed on the next generation through a *postmortem ad personam* will. Saving the liberal discretionality of a living person, without the need to recourse to taxation, there are ways to rethink the process of perpetuating some inequalities.

I would point out two more proposals in this respect. One is to always keep diachrony in mind. I have always thought that the social contract of which Rousseau spoke is nothing more than an entelechy, but speaking in that tone, as a form of wishful thinking, as illusions that it would be nice if they had happened, if there had been some kind of social contract, that contract should have been given between generations. That is diachrony: to think that we coexist in time with generations that are outside of time. Diachrony is lived fundamentally in the family, and it is what allows, as we have said, the enriching relationship between grandparents and grandchildren.

The other proposal is a theme that I have dealt with in depth in several writings, and that is community. Without community, society cannot be understood. Society is a collection of communities, and all of us belong to many at the same time. To understand, to give public visibility to the community, seems tremendously necessary to free ourselves. Not forever, because nothing is forever in our history, but to free ourselves, I say, from those perverse effects that individualism has had and has in our culture.

And *thirdly*, we must also speak of the challenge represented by the need to prevent the multiplication of power structures. The end of modernity has been characterized by a notable increase in structural power that fundamentally affects three areas to which I must refer. The first is the environmental sphere. Here it seems necessary to articulate planetary rights that preserve biodiversity and ensure some kind of climate stability and, from the point of view of economics, incorporate the externality in the price. The state, the now existing powers, have to act in the market to make this feasible. We see no other way than to incorporate waste into the market on account of prices. One has to pay for one's waste, for one's fumes, as an effective way of discouraging depredation. The second is to rethink the states in extension. We are referring to the decisive relationship between state and territory, which seems to me to be already exhausted. I would like to see on the horizon some discussions on the viability of nonterritorial states, in the hope that in the not too distant future each of us would not be obliged to hold citizenship of the territory in which we were born, but that citizenship could be chosen to the extent that, in addition to territorial states, there would also be nonterritorial states. And thirdly, beyond rethinking states in extension, it is also necessary to rethink states in intensity. I am referring to desacralization, which we will discuss in the final chapter. There is a very interesting element there that has to do with religious freedom, and that is that the state must imitate the church, which has already separated from the state. Now it is the state that should do its own *mea culpa* to separate itself from the sacred. This is what I call the Fourth Christianity. By secularizing the situation of the states, they must renounce, or we must make them renounce, their sacred powers. It does not seem, at this point in history, that it is necessary for states to worship or be worshipped.

Biological identity, the bad inheritance of individualism, and the structures of power—in particular, those that threaten the environment and those that preserve the privileges of the territorial states constituted as such—are three main reflections that, in my opinion, we must ask ourselves at the change of eras. What means do we have to take up these challenges, to shore up this incorrectness (that which makes them sound bad from the modern point of view)? Well, the fundamental means is our freedom and its consequence in self-mastery with which we can endow ourselves to prevent the empire of other people's dominions. To prevent these dominions from turning us into their subjects, their slaves, it is necessary not only to decommodify, to remove from the market many things that do not have to be there, but also to depoliticize, to remove from the sphere of political decision many things that do not have to be there and that belong more to civility or to the family.

In my opinion, to the extent that we reduce the coercive power of the market that incorporates us as addicted consumers through dubious access (for example, the sale of our data by computer monopolies), we will be freer and more capable of self-control. Consequently, to the extent that areas or possibilities of self-mastery are consolidated, we will be able to sow transcendent aspirations. One of the great evils of our time is cultural apathy, which leads to a culture of discouragement. The increase in suicide rates is astonishing many societies supposedly freed from material scarcity, and in view of this there is a need to open channels for religiosity so that we become aware that there is also a spiritual dimension to the human. Certainly, this is something that may seem difficult to concretize, but it is urgent to give it a channel.

This critique that we are implicitly making of modernity, even at certain points from within modernity, is by no means a critique of totality. There are treasures that we ought to save from collapse, and I would like to point out three to conclude this chapter. In the first place, tradition must be rescued. We have already mentioned that social contract between generations that confirms diachrony and that we can also call tradition, but specifically, we are referring now to the need to affirm culture over situational logics, over procedural logics, and this implies recognizing and valuing shared reasons. To rescue an epistemology of trust and to value knowledge over certainties and slogans; to value life as a course instead of valuing moments; and to value beauty instead of valuing utility. Culture is an accumulated baggage over the centuries that gives us a referent quality of identity.

Secondly, in addition to rescuing tradition through the affirmation of culture over customary, inertial, and formal logics, it will be necessary to rescue intelligence so that reason can be affirmed over cultures. I am referring to those cultures in the form of fashions imposed by political correctness (we note the incoherence of calling these fashions culture). It is a matter of putting aside these corrections to save reason. A reason that points to provisional truths and that necessarily has to do with the discourse that each one makes, the interpretation that each one perceives of the situation in which he lives. Earlier, we pointed out the immense richness of the qualifier "human." It is true that we are cultural beings, but there is a rational sanction that sometimes needs to be updated so that inhumanity does not creep in.

And finally, we must rescue excellence to the extent that we can concretize it by affirming virtues over values. Virtues are personalized excellences, and it is necessary that these virtues become visible so that testimonies of exemplarity, of heroic exemplarity, can be given, even in post-heroic times, which demand more virtue than strength. Many modern people are full of mouths talking and proposing values, but if those values do not land in virtuous lives, they are carried away by the wind of demagogy. Yes, it is about nothing more and nothing less than being better. An excellence within the reach of anyone at any time.

We are not elaborating any civil or political program. The new era that is coming is not an era, as the post-liberals have said, in which politics will be understood in a different way but maintaining the channels that modernity has given birth to. Nor does yours truly believe that the permanence of representative channels is desirable so that communicative action can develop according to the canons of supposedly elitist elucidation. The coming era will be simpler and more transparent, and it would not be a bad thing to bring power down to the street level, with a commitment to affable rupture as opposed to the continuity of a past monopolized by ideological sectarianism of one or the other sign. There is no need to hand out cards and titles representative of anyone if everyone can be a representative of himself, individually or as a family. It is the people who should dialogue and pact, not the ideologies.

Politics, certainly, will have to be understood in a different way so that there will be much less politics, and in this sense we will be much more the protagonists of this new era that is dawning. The game is played on someone else's field, but the opponent is demoralized and out of age. Let us free ourselves from the insecurity complex that can make us look longingly at old failed states, and let us bet on saving the new man from the superiority complexes that dulled the existence of the old one.

Thus, the change must be two-fold: technical and tactical. Inside with a virtuous training and outside with a new sense of perception of the public: preparation and disposition; to understand oneself capable and to be where one should be. Hence, where we must begin to change is by ourselves, opening wide our minds to assimilate a friendly goodbye to a journey of uncertain discovery. Goodbye, modernity, and thank you for what we have received.

11. The City

THE CITY IS NOT innocent. On the contrary, it is one of the main aggressors against the environment, and the excessive growth of some of them mortgages us all. The rural-urban relationship seems to have been broken. This makes it necessary to imagine livable and healthy cities and an inhabited rural environment. These are the hallmarks of a new way of understanding life.

Many years ago, I had the privileged gift of teaching a subject in the faculty of economics in the old curricula of French heritage, which included one called "Rural and Urban Sociology," a subject that has obviously disappeared from the faculty since, like most of the subjects that have to do with sociology. The compartmentalization of knowledge in the university has these malicious consequences. However, the study of the city is something that belongs to economics as it does to anthropology and sociology. It has a multidisciplinary object of study and is also a necessary and highly topical object of study. We are witnesses that in the last one hundred years there has been a remarkable change in the life of human beings on the planet, and that is that we have gone from 9 percent to more than 50 percent urban population. In other times this could be something that had nothing to do with the future of life, but right now, unfortunately, it has a lot to do with it.

Cities today have become dangerous, and I am not referring to safety but, more fundamentally, to the environment. The city has become a polluting agent par excellence, to the point that it has become necessary for many of the people who live in the city (and many politicians as well) to rethink themselves as "citizens." There is pertinent talk of the need to re-ruralize, to disperse ourselves. We are too concentrated and poorly distributed on the planet, and we are realizing this now, when certain risky behaviors, certain consumptions and wastes, and certain diseases are making themselves felt. But we are also facing a conceptual problem, because life in the city has turned us into inhabitants of artificial environments. The difference between the rural and the urban, between the countryside and the city, is calibrated around the natural/artificial axis, and the city is seen as an artificial environment in which human beings must necessarily feel uncomfortable.

If we examine what has happened in the last one hundred years with the great urbanizing process, we find a variety of transitions from the rural to the urban. We cannot speak of a process of urbanization but rather *processes* of urbanization, because they are very diverse. Thus, we cannot say that urbanization is a consequence of modernization. They occur at the same time. We neither see a cause-effect relationship between them nor do we think that there is a preeminent cause-effect relationship between urbanization and industrialization.

There are great thinkers who have devoted time and research to the study of the city and some particularly important ones in sociology. We can think of Ferdinand Tönnies, who distinguishes between community and association. For Tönnies, what marks this distinction is the urbanizing process. Before the megacity, the community was more present in human relations. Since then, it has been replaced by association. This shift from community to association is a leap that points conceptually to individualism. One of the most negative consequences of the great urbanizing process that human beings have undergone in the last one hundred years is precisely the scourge of individualism.

The city is a produced space. Some of those who have studied the subject say that this space is dependent on an economic system. I believe that there has been a very important relationship between the economy and the urbanization process, but this relationship has also existed with technological development and urbanization, with face-to-face education, and between health and new medicines and urbanization. In the urbanization process there has also been an important relationship between the city and leisure. It is more complex than it seems.

We have talked about great thinkers who have dedicated themselves to this subject and we have mentioned only one, but there are more. Whoever is up to date and has been concerned about life in the city and how it has changed and evolved, or what its impact is on human anthropology, will be aware of the work of Richard Sennett and his *homo faber* trilogy: *The Craftsman* (2008), *Together* (2012), and *Building and Dwelling* (2019). But previously, Sennett had written *Flesh and Stone* (1997) and *Human Life and Personal Identity* (2001). Apart from Sennett, one must also necessarily mention an author whom one likes very much but seems to be a bit forgotten in the references and in the modern bibliography: Lewis Mumford, who wrote in *The Culture of Cities* (1945). And, of course, we must remember the Chicago school (the sociological, neither the economic nor the architectural), which focuses precisely on the study of the city. One has had the privilege of spending a research stay there, and among its authors, we must point out the master-and-disciple duo of Robert Park, who wrote *The City* (1925), and Amos Hawley, who wrote *Human Ecology* (1950). The terms *human ecology* and *social ecology* come from the Chicago school and are now used particularly when studying the development and expansion of cities.

About the city, we can ask ourselves if it has something to do with the end of modernity. Certainly, the urban explosion and the abandonment of land have something to do with each other, but I don't think there is a causal relationship. It should be noted that we have gone from the demolition of walls to the invasion of nature. The city has defeated the countryside, but it has defeated the countryside at a great price for all of us. Still, in our imaginary, those ancient dichotomies that have to do with the birth of modernity between citizen and villain, between the domestic and the savage, the cultured and the crude, survive. The citizen was the term used by the leaders of the French Revolution; the citizen, I say, was the person who was worthwhile. Now, in countries where there is a national identity card, the place of birth is used as a way of knowing whether one comes from the city or from the town and countryside, leaving a dichotomous aftertaste in the cultural imaginary. But if this was so, it will no longer be so. We are beginning to see the citizen as an aggressor and not as a savior. The city is the highest polluting subject among those that make up human groups. The city produces garbage, pollution, and an immense volume of externality that is not assumed by itself. And this is a major turning point when it comes to thinking about a livable future.

Seeing cities as aggressors of the environment and citizens, at the same time, as victims of their city and as agents of external aggression, has changed the panorama. The mortgage that large cities place on the future of the countries in which they are located is immense. The challenge is how we can solve these problems and stop the city from being a serious blight on the future of humanity. There is no other way than to rethink it, and with some urgency.

There are two points that I would dare to suggest to put on the agenda of reconstruction, first mentally and then practically. The first is that cities must assume their externality like any other subject. That is, they must assume, mainly, their waste, garbage, and the cost of pollution, and this, in my opinion, can be done economically from one day to the next. I am not advocating a collection of extra taxes on those who live in the city, but by means of indirect incentives, it would be possible to make those externalities that are not assumed now, to be assumed. Naturally, it is proposed to end the throwaway culture or the use of non-recyclable materials (such as plastic and the externality of planned obsolescence), which includes a severe education at the expense of the pocket: whoever pollutes should pay by personalizing the cost where they live.

And the other point is that cities should assume their demographic cost politically. This is already done in some countries, where the vote in the countryside is worth more than the vote in the city. This can be organized in a simple way in those political systems that have single-person representation seats, where each territory has its only representative in the chamber or parliament.

We have talked about re-ruralization, and we think that these two measures would help to implement it, through dynamics of demographic reversion from the city to the town or countryside. We must be clear about this: we cannot think of a city for the future with unsustainable growth. And I am not referring to economic growth but to demographic growth. We should distribute ourselves better and take the necessary indirect measures to make living in small towns or cities attractive again. In some countries and contexts this is, moreover, urgent and necessary.

Apart from these dynamics of reversion in large cities, a network of small cities must be articulated to revitalize life in rural areas. We have already mentioned Erick Fritz Schumacher, who founded the Intermediate Technology Development Group in 1969 (now called Practical Action, since 2005), which has, as one of its missions, proposed to make city life healthier. Well, the idea of the German-British thinker was to make an economy as if people mattered for something. Thus, the idea is to reconvert and make cities as if the people who live in them mattered and as if the environment were a treasure to be preserved and cared for.

One of the scourges that we now observe among young people is the inability to distinguish between the artifice of nature and the virtuality of reality, to which we will return in another chapter. We should change this confusion of realities, this progressive distancing from the natural, to allow for a more humane civic life. We are committed to the real as opposed to the unreal and to the healthy as opposed to the harmful. There is a challenge here, not only for thinkers or politicians but for all of us, because perhaps we are the ones who vote with our feet when it comes to revitalizing life in the countryside. Moving out of the city is now more possible than ever before thanks to new technologies. This may be a viable option for many of us, and we may consider it soon.

12. Democracy

WE MAKE HERE A defense of skeptical democracy and self-mastery as well as a warning about the dangers of understanding democracy as an end in itself. Democracy is, at least it seems to us, a process, not a stable state, and its end is external to politics. Hence, its study and examination must involve several disciplines.

It is a difficult subject to deal with from a sociological point of view. To the extent that one enters into it, it must be treated with a certain suspicion, and we say suspicion because of the adjectives. The concept of democracy has many adjectives, and when one sees so many and such contradictory adjectives, it is logical to be suspicious. We have seen it labeled as liberal—that which operates without any prerequisite other than age and involves the division of powers—but there is also the guilder, corporate, organic, or institutional, which somewhat limit access to what we call parity election; aristocratic democracies, which may be a derivation and implementation of technocracy; meritocracy, more or less hierarchical, or something that involves a difference in status *ab initio*; digital democracy, so fashionable today, in which there is no parliament and in which direct democracy is practiced; qualified democracy, insofar as the sphere or space occupied by the seat in the representation is more or less qualified; plebiscitary democracy, in which acclamation replaces election; censorious democracy, in which certain conditions are set to belong to the census of voters; and there are those who speak of sentimental democracy. In short, there is such a wide range of adjectives that one starts to get lost when one begins to reflect on democracy, and even more so today, when democracy is hijacked and questioned, one thinks, with good reason.

We are witnessing so many problems as the democratic experience is reproducing throughout the world that sometimes there is no choice but to take refuge or resort to suspicion. There is a particularly interesting book written by Colin Crouch entitled *Post-Democracy* (2000). The author, writing from the perspective of the left, attributes the defects of democracy to the lack of interest in political participation, the ability of certain opinion media to manipulate the masses, and the closed elites that control communication and even produce castes from the political point of view. In the end, the author questions whether democracy is possible in environments where there is neither participation nor equality. If we turn to a more or less classical thinker, Hannah Arendt, who is much cited these days, we see that the author puts her finger on the sore point when she says that without truth there is no democracy and, even more so, in contexts where there is talk of the knowledge society where, it seems, there is so much knowledge of the same things that are incompatible with each other.

But we may ask ourselves, is it possible to detect truth and truths in today's so-called knowledge society? Communication being central and basic to the transmission of content, and knowing that there is nothing more manipulable than communication, how can it be said that truth is the basis of democracy? Arendt argues that today there is no need to lie to the people to protect them, something that comes from Plato. But on the contrary, we see that lying is very much present in democratic practice, especially considering that false information is 70 percent more likely to be shared on networks than true information.

All this is something we should consider before proposing democracy without adjectives. We should also consider issues such as the digital divide, which separates some people from others in terms of communication. We can also think of the importance of the predominance of the image, of the peripheral, over content, when it comes to pointing out the problems that beset democracy, and, why not, speak of the predominance of emotivism over rationality or of the consumer society of the democratic spectacle. All these are nothing more than drawbacks, and pointing to what Arendt said that without truth there is no democracy, how can access to truth be achieved?

Some say that truth is the result of consensus (it is not usually pointed out among whom), which entails adding to the list of obstacles and inconveniences the dangers derived from the denunciation of relativism or useful "truths." On the other hand, what about post-truth, disinformation, or misinformation? Is it consensual by discerning or discriminating sources, or not? Well, we see that the subject is sufficiently complex for us to reflect slowly, so I am going to try to make a more personalized reflection in which I include opinions, sustained in my publications, defending a skeptical democracy, a democracy that should not be a goal but a process to which we will arrive by mediating four basic questions, which I believe we should ask ourselves from the outset when reflecting on the subject.

The first two questions have to do with the subject. The first would be that of the active subject, and the second that of the passive subject from the point of view of the whom. As regards the active subject, we must ask ourselves who governs me and whom I govern. We are all governed by many people. Someone at work is governed by his boss, someone on the road is governed by the traffic wardens and the traffic laws, someone at home is governed by whoever is in charge at home, the neighbor is governed by the community of neighbors, and we are all governed in some way by everyone. Who do I govern? No one, if possible, and the fewer the better. Because this is the question of self-control, my self-control and the self-control of others must be respected to the maximum.

The other question that has to do with the subject is that of the passive subject, and the question there is the question of the sovereign. When speaking of the passive subject, we remember Abraham Lincoln's expression: of the people, for the people, and by the people. But who is the sovereign people? The question is very difficult to answer. I am also a sovereign subject, and if several of us get together to live self-sufficiently, we can become another sovereign subject. But we ought to start from reality, and reality is made of superimposed sovereignties. From the communitarian point of view, in which one moves, each community has its own sovereignty, and each sovereignty has its rules, functions, and forms. There is a basic collectivity which is the family, another collectivity is the neighborhood, another collectivity or community is my professional association, my religious affiliation, etc. All these communities, so to speak, have their own sovereignty. Thus, we consider the self as a passive subject, but, more importantly, my different selves as passive subjects as well. This is very interesting because if each of us belongs to many communities at the same time, then each of us is answerable to many sovereigns of which each of us is also a part.

The other two questions that remain to be asked are the how and the where. The question that usually immediately arises about the how is whether maximum or minimum democracy, direct democracy, or representative democracy, and, in any case, from the theoretical point of view, the less representation and the more participation, the better. As we have already discussed, one does not have to appoint a representative when one can do it oneself. In every area in which democracy operates, we can raise this question, which is becoming increasingly relevant due to the possibilities opened by communication technologies.

But the where is, in our opinion, the most pressing question today. It is the question of where democracy should operate. Should it operate exclusively in the political sphere or also in the social and economic spheres? Should there be democracy in families, in companies, in the civil sphere, in the religious sphere, or in the institutional sphere? These are questions that we must stop to think about before continuing to talk about democracy. Here, for reasons of space and tone, we are not going to dwell on them, but we will leave them listed, although you can guess our position advocating a functional democracy that should not put the concept on a pedestal so that it does not hinder hierarchies (we should not be afraid of this word) more functional or with more rights in certain areas.

In the questions of the subject of to whom and from whom, in the question of how, and in the question of where, there underlies, as it could not be otherwise, the issue of power. The point of view that I defend is that ideally, we should all fight, in a metaphorical sense of course, to defend our own sovereignty, to defend our self-control (also in the plural), from interference by various powers. The first thing is to stand up against unjust power, against the power that assumes dominion over me and us without me (or us) having given it to them, and consequently, after this rejection of dominating powers, to organize the remains. In these remains is a hidden treasure that is my freedom and our shared freedoms in the different communities in which one is who one is. The accumulation of power has always been denounced as the most undemocratic thing that exists, and indeed it is.

Democracy is not an accumulation but a dispersion of power. It is, or should be, an expeditious way through which power reaches the people. It is a vehicle, so to speak, with an expression that I do not like very much, empowering, and that is why we say that democracy is a process and not a state. Freedom is here a consequence. From the practical point of view, when we review history, freedom comes after having questioned power. First it is power, to reject the dominions of which one is a slave, and then to affirm freedom and, concretely, to say that we must dominate ourselves in order to be free, to dominate ourselves in order not to dominate anyone, and to dominate ourselves so that no one dominates us. To that extent, each of us, with the several "us" that conform who we are, will be free. Thus, I believe that those who confine democracy to the practice of voting, which can protect, for example, a dictatorship of the majorities, know nothing of democracy.

Democracy, it has been said, implies the division of powers that we have already mentioned when speaking of liberal democracy, but it also implies respect, tolerance, civility, and subsidiarity. Democracy is a path that should lead to empowerment, to the self-mastery of political communities and various subjects. It is a path of dispersion of power, which enables sovereignty, which makes sovereign those who were not sovereign before or were not aware of being so. That is why it is so difficult to define democracy. It is not a state, it is a process. This is capital. When somebody has put, metaphorically speaking, a gun to my chest to give a definition of democracy, I have ended up saying that it is "the participation and collective decision in the management of the public by those concerned," always saving the right, the freedoms, and the realities of departure. Democracy is a means, not an end. The end can be peace, justice, welfare, harmony, freedom, or progress, hence whoever thinks that democracy is an end has a lot of formalistic illusion and, at worst, is someone who sees democracy as a vehicle to monopolize power for himself and his own.

I conclude the chapter. If war is the failure of politics, politics is the failure of civility. From what I have said, it will come as no surprise that I call for democracy to be skeptical of itself. There are many people today, also in academic life, who are full of mouths talking about the truths of democracy. Yes, democracy is something positive and rich; it is good, but it is a path. What is really important is the goal of that path. Let us be very careful of putting democracy in such a high place, so high, so high, so high, from which we cannot get anywhere.

13. Borders

ALWAYS, BEHIND A BORDER there is another one. They are part of reality, and it is better to recognize, understand, and propose them than to ignore them. Any diversity and plurality presuppose them, originating the multiverse in which we recognize ourselves as humans.

This chapter has a certain relationship with other themes we have already dealt with, such as the limit, but the border adds a new and very interesting imaginary. Apart from the fact that it is a theme that has permeated sociology and anthropological research, we are going to try to make a certain defense of the border from the conceptual point of view, which, in our opinion, should also be reflected in practice. The need to recognize borders is present in our minds. Thus, the border, in our perception, has to be conceptualized in the plural. We are made up of borders that may be spatial, in my opinion the least important, but there are also cultural borders, which usually get a bad press. These are sometimes presented as an obstacle to equality, but curiously enough, we must begin by saying that without borders there is no equality possible. The border, in a way, is what marks the subject, the subject of equality and the subject of difference.

Having made this generic statement, we could say that what we are going to deal with in this chapter is, at the same time, the marking and unmarking of frontiers. There is now a proliferation of those who call themselves borderless, as if that were possible. Apart from the better-known doctors without borders, there are also clowns without borders, reporters without borders, cooks without borders, etc. However, borders are in the reality of life, in fact, to the same extent that we recognize ourselves as different and recognize that there are others, that there is another; there, we mark a border.

Life itself is a frontier with death and everything that is other, everything that is not me, everything that is not us, everything that is different, and everything that is alternative marked by a frontier. Borders can be spatial, as

135

we say the least important, but there are also social borders, religious borders, ethnic borders, and linguistic borders, which are now especially on the rise, and in our discipline, in sociology, there is a sociology of the border. From the border, there is a study that has a certain history in anthropology and cultural sociology, which is the study of frontier countries, those who realize themselves in their conquest. I had the opportunity to go into this field some time ago, studying the comparative case between two countries that were frontier societies, such as Australia and Argentina.

There is a starting point here, and it is that in the debate that arises between unity and plurality, the conceptualization of the frontier is perfectly compatible with unity. For this writer, borders are permeable, they are changeable, they can overlap, they are flexible, but they must exist and we must recognize them. Borders are compatible with unity, the unity of the human race and the unity of institutions. They are also compatible with diversity, with the plurality that makes up affinities. To the extent that institutions incorporate and institutions separate, this does not go against equality, because this very separation is what allows us to speak of equality and inequality. Without separation, there are no subjects from which any equality or inequality can be practiced.

It is perhaps in the political imaginary where the border issue has been treated with the greatest suspicion. Speaking, above all, of distributive justice, the justification of mutual duty within the border is what ultimately justifies the singularity of state coercion. The border would mark that dividing line between what belongs to a state and what is outside the state, and there, distributive justice marks duties and rights that bind some who are in one place and do not bind others who are outside, not only geographically but in another space with cultural distinction. The border, from this point of view in the political imaginary, creates binding citizens—citizens who have rights and duties among themselves.

Many of the theorists who have articulated a political theory based on the frontier have tended, and this seems to me to be a mistake, have tended, I say, to equate society and state insofar as the contrast between state coercion and personal autonomy is based on the laws that make up the legal framework of the state. Among these thinkers, we can include leading figures in political thought, such as John Rawls himself, William Blake, or David Miller. It is something that is very present in the argument of the liberal political imaginary, especially in Anglo-Saxon countries. Outside and beyond the political imaginary, closer to us, we have the social imaginary, and in the social imaginary there is a danger when arguing the frontier— that is, the supposed identification between state and identity. One of the great obstacles we have now to understand each other and one of the most important sources of conflict in the world is the lack of understanding of identity, which is often understood in the singular but I prefer to understand in the plural. Identity is plural because, among other things, as a communitarian, I believe that we all belong to many communities at the same time.

We act more and more in spaces that, by definition, have no borders, as is the case of the Internet, and here we must refer again to a great man to whom we often do not pay enough attention: Marshall McLuhan and his *The Global Village*. McLuhan pointed out the distinction between the frontier and the line of separation, something that is understood more in English than in Spanish, because there are two words, frontier and boundary, to differentiate. In Spanish when we speak of frontier, we think more of the borderline. The frontier we are talking about here is not only the borderline but, more importantly, that conceptual frontier that makes us think of ourselves as diverse and group ourselves diversely.

I usually say that there is an error when it comes to thinking about the frontier and that is the totalization of social reality as a uniform globalized whole in which any type of diversity could fit or should fit and be integrated. I am not in favor of globalism because, among other things, I think that our world is an encapsulated world, and that, beyond the frontier, there is always another one.

The unknown, however strange or mysterious, is not empty. The conquest of the American West or the so-called Argentinean desert wars were in fact the extension of one frontier at the expense of another. There are no vacuums and even less so in this world where frontiers now fill everything. There is no promised land waiting for us beyond the mountains. We are what we are, and we are where we are. That is why I dislike the use of the term "metaverse" and I do not like the term "universe." I prefer to talk about "multiverse" because it refers to those multiple identities that each of us have. Identities are born fundamentally in community. We all belong to diverse communities, and beyond the moldable borders that make up group identities, there are also individual identities. I am the unique sum of my community identities, of my *wes*.

We have talked before about the world being encapsulated. It is a world that is full of diverse frontiers, and this links us reciprocally. The danger, and here I understand those who view the border with suspicion and speak of borders as something dangerous, the danger, I say, is not in the fact that borders exist but in that equivalence that many place between state and monopolistic identity and, consequently, in the fight or struggle between states to reaffirm their identity (moving it from the imaginary to the real) by assuming a greater share of power and establishing it forever. This is the great scourge of human history. A reciprocally linked world in which states compete is a world that is only appeased by fear and suspicion, if not worse. If the neighbor has an army, I must have one too; if the neighbor has armaments, so must I. The escalation of armaments is justified. The escalation of armaments is justified here in protection, but today, in the atomic age, it lacks any rational justification.

How can we go from a situation in which the state protagonism has taken over the border discourse to the point of living in perpetuity under an atomic threat? Does it justify taking the risk? Some think that the solution lies in making border conglomerates rather than putting states in competition with each other, replacing state rivalries with pluri-state rivalries. It was argued that atomic disarmament and moratoriums could coexist with the reason of these pluri-states. But other diverse planetary challenges appeared, such as the ecological one, which immediately overcame the rationality of this new frontier of confrontation. No, borders are not the danger, the danger lies in how we perceive them, especially one type of border: the territorial border that frames what we call the national or pluralist state.

Thus, the danger to come, in my opinion, is the states, not the borders and not the communities. We are frontier; the human being is a frontier. The universe, ours if there are no others, is matter that expands in the time through which we pass. When it comes to interpreting and reflecting on the frontier, I think it is very healthy to think that we pass through time and not the other way around. The quasi-infinite referentiality that our passage through time implies endows us with multiple identities that make up the existing multiverse, which gives reason for life, which is reality.

It is all very complex but challenging. There are many frontiers, and some are imposing and dangerous, but the eagerness of some to dispense with all of them, to share everything in a uniform world empty of personal or collective identities, seems to me to be a serious mistake. Here we have tried to bet on the border, to give it a leading role, to understand it. This is a major disciplinary challenge for both political theory and sociology. We spoke earlier of marking and unmarking, and in that paradox we conclude. To affirm borders in order to relativize states, giving primacy to social dynamics over political statics, *domus* over *polis*. It is a matter of making flexible but not liquid, approaches that have conditioned human relations within constituted societies and international politics, in search, always, of understandings that prevent conflicts and wars without achieving it completely.

14. Finitude

IN AN APOCALYPTIC AND dystopian era such as ours, it is inevitable to wonder whether or not we will be at the end of an era or at the end of time. After an analysis of different perspectives, we arrive at what seem to us to be the two successful concepts of the present moment: acceleration and presentism and, within this, the viability or not of a future mortgaged by atomic radiation.

I must remember, as always, that we are making a reflection from sociology without undermining the contribution of other disciplines, and, in this one on finitude, there are many interesting ones. Thus, for example, philosophy. The Spaniards Luis Duch and Joan-Carles Melich have warned us about the convenience of inhabiting spaces and no longer just walking through them. The ambiguities of love illustrate the terror and tyranny of time and Melich in particular, in *Filosofía de la finitud*, speaks to us of the brevity of life, of the surprising fact of brevity, which raises the question of what for. From existentialism we have been reminded that to live is not only to be, but mostly to exist, that nothing happens because nothing happens to me, and that experience is an event, a realization. That is why existence commits forgiveness, also to others. It has a relational dimension: existing with others involves me and involves them. These approaches, which emerge, for example, from Martin Heidegger's *Being and Time* or Jean-Paul Sartre's *Being and Nothingness*, have enlightened thinkers from different disciplines on finitude.

Edgar Morin, in *Man and Death*, speaks of the relationship between this revolt in the face of death and the rise of individualism. Anthropology, on the other hand, has dealt with the phenomenon of some funerary cults, insofar as these cults are a collective thinking about death that permeates and shapes differentiated cultures. Recently, studies have appeared on the cult of death in Mexico or on the cult of *San-la-muerte* in Argentina. The political eschatologies of Marxism, of liberalism, in the case of Francis

Fukuyama, as well as theological eschatologies, are very much to the point. All three have enlightened us on the future and present us with paradises to come if we follow the recipes they propose. Nowadays, a Gnostic millenarianism is in vogue, which has taken hold in some Protestant sects or ex-sects and some sectors of North American evangelicalism. It is not surprising that, in relation to this, modern cinematography presents us with so many films about a dystopian future.

But, as we have said, we wanted to approach the reflection on finitude from our discipline, from sociology, and perhaps the first thing we should do is to bring up the contribution of a master. That master is Robert Nisbet, who wrote in the second half of the twentieth century a very important work called *History of the Idea of Progress*. In it, the North American author wonders what is the reason for the rise of contemporary skepticism. That weariness that has been generated in modernity to the point of considering that we are in its final stage. He points out four causes for the rise of skepticism in this epochal finitude, namely: the limits to economic development, natural and resource limits, the limits of scientific analysis and the end of a methodology that has given us many opportunities to progress, and, finally, the weariness of the abundance of material goods and spiritual recipes of today for tomorrow. These four causes produce, according to him, the contemporary skepticism that points to an end of cycle. What will it bring us and what will come next? Nisbet says at the end of his book that the idea of progress could disappear by means of a thermonuclear holocaust, and with the disappearance of the idea of progress, almost all of us would disappear. But it may also not disappear, and for this second possibility to occur, he points to a revitalization of religion. Religious revival can fill the void left by modernity.

It is an interesting reflection on finitude. There is now an effervescence in sociology on this subject. A lot is being written and not in vain. This is due to some of the concepts with which we sociologists operate. In addition to the idea of progress, we have the theme of development, and, concomitantly with it, the concept of sustainability. There is also the treatment of the subject from the field of socioeconomics and the dilemma between growth or degrowth. From the same perspective and from the more strictly economic sphere, there is talk of expectation. We realize, perhaps to some surprise, how it is that mere expectation increases the value of products and issues that suddenly become fashionable and their value rises exponentially without ceasing to be what they were before.

In this respect, it is worth focusing attention on life expectancy. A subject we have dealt with in *Sociología del Desarrollo Sostenible* (2005) or *Sociology of Sustainable Development* and in *Sociedad y Medio Ambiente*

(1997) or *Society and Environment*. There is a big change in considering and working with life expectancy. I have criticized the concept and use of average life expectancy, which says very little about a population. It is true that there is a big difference between a country with a life expectancy of more than eighty years and a country with an average life expectancy of less than sixty, but when we examine what this difference means, what we find is that in one country there are more social inequalities than in another and little else. Now we are also working on healthy life expectancy, autonomous life expectancy, and life expectancy after the age of sixty. I have worked on life expectancy from the moment of conception, and there are also those who talk about social life expectancy. Moreover, there is a novel approach, which studies life expectancy not by studying humans but by studying the supports of humans. We talk about geological and cosmological life expectancy and how they affect the shaping of our behaviors. Knowing that we are on a planet that is not eternal, that we are facing a star that also expires, and that in principle this expiration has no prospect of being replaced has given rise to a very interesting sub-discipline, which is the sociology of time.

There is a reference here to the classics, to this type of analysis, and, in the first place, to Durkheim, but also to Alfred Schultz and, more recently, to Norbert Elias, who have worked on the relationship that capitalism may have had with the use of time, with how we distribute our time, and how this has permeated cultures in which the relationship between age and occupation, the relationship between age and rites of passage, life cycles, changes in schedules, and, lately, how certain human groups are living at night and how some urban tribes are more involved in it than in the daytime.

Another theme dear to the sociology of time is the analysis of social times, of cyclical routines, of times that are periodically reserved for festivities, for collective rites of passage, and also for jubilees. The classics have considered this mutant relationship between economy, culture, and society, and how the long-standing validity of capitalism has shaped and transformed us. What will come next? It seems obvious that modernity is coming to an end, the end of an era, but the ability to predict is required of any scientist. With the social sciences, that ability has been reduced to a minimum, due to the exponential increase of social changes operating in society as a whole. However, there are two issues within the reflection on finitude and starting from the sociology of time that are of particular interest when it comes to daring to predict.

One is the issue of acceleration. There is a German author who has studied it very well, Hartmut Rosa, who from the so-called critical theory has analyzed the relationship between acceleration and alienation. We refer to the acceleration of technology, to the speed with which we move through the day and through the years and through space. Acceleration has changed us. It has changed our habits, our expectations, and the way we conduct ourselves. The question we ask is whether that acceleration is going to be able to keep up with us, because if we are at the end of an epoch and at the end of that epoch, we are going too fast, at worst we will crash.

Before reaching the next epoch, we are presented with the dilemma of whether we have to do something to change the epoch, whether we have to do something to get out of modernity: what we have to do to look at it from the rear-view mirror. Perhaps, as a precautionary measure, we ought to slow down, stop, or change vehicles. Maybe we ought to leave, run away from the old us. We will not be able to do this if at the same time we drive as fast as we have been driving collectively. Especially considering, as we will see later, that this change of era in the making and how we conduct ourselves in it, in some way, may condition it to be the last one.

The other issue is that of presentism. We understand presentism as a conscious forgetting of the past and the future to focus on the present. A forgetfulness that seems irresponsible as it does not consider the deferred effects over time of our actions and, fundamentally, this points to a problem that in my opinion, already stated, is very important and to which we are not paying enough attention: the problem of the atomic age. Presentism makes us forgetful of the inconveniences and damages that we leave for later, of nuclear waste and of the problems that may arise from the proliferation of the use of atomic energy. We are consuming more and more energy, and we wonder if it is necessary. We are faced with a growing demand, a growing dependence on atomic energy, which necessarily leads to mortgaging the future of humanity for thousands of years to come. The destructive potential of nuclear waste storage is immeasurable, to the point that only from a cosmic perspective can we realize the damage it can cause.

Many authors have led to divide the history of mankind into two halves, one until 1945 and the other after that date, after the first use of the atomic bomb by the United States of America on the cities of Nagasaki and Hiroshima. Atomic energy may seem to us to be a need for cheap energy, but it is an illusory need in both senses: that it may not be so necessary for us to consume so much energy, and that it is not so cheap considering the externality.

Acceleration and presentism bring us back to those questions we have been asking ourselves. First, will modernity drag us to its end, as the first civilization capable of global self-destruction? We can self-destruct, and there may be those who are consciously so modern, so modern, so modern, that in order not to terminate modernity they will terminate humanity. It is a danger, and we know that there may be a person crazy enough for that.

The perspective of stopping the car and saying to modernity—we have come this far—seems a feasible and advisable perspective. From academia, from science, it is an obligation, in my opinion, to raise this question in its crudest terms.

Reflection on finitude is not exhausted here. Apart from what has been said about direct destruction, indirect destruction also threatens historical continuity. The destruction of our vital support in the environment hinders the vision of a possible future. Ecological survival necessarily implies reflection on the viability of the present system of production and consumption, and in order to consider its possible replacement, it is necessary to turn to the economy.

Thus, when talking about future scenarios, in my opinion, we can speak of four main ones. The first of these could be called *volitional optimism*. This is the scenario of those who think that nature is self-regulating and that, without being denialists from the point of view of environmental issues, they think that we cannot fix anything that goes against the survival of nature. They think that nature, unlike us, will take care of it. This forced optimism takes society out of nature, which seems to us to be an untenable premise. Nature and society are intrinsically linked to the point that we have argued for the social character of nature. Volitional optimism is also very dear to those who defend the survival of the current system of production and consumption.

A second possible scenario that we can contemplate is that of *eco-fascism*. A universal dictatorship of ecological character that defends the interference in certain countries and that would result from the consideration that the environmental problem can finish with us. To solve this problem, given the perceived incompetence of human societies to solve it by themselves, the only possibility that appears is that power acts to ensure that countries and institutions respect the minimum regulations that ensure survival.

A third scenario is that of *collective euthanasia*, defended by those who, living in the most unsupportive presentism, think that it is not worthwhile to guarantee life to future generations to maintain the standard of living of the present generation. There are even supporters of collective euthanasia who have calculated the optimal number of future generations that should populate the planet, after which a programmed self-destruction should be considered.

And the fourth future scenario we would consider is that of the *new ecological paradigm* (NEP). The NEP would support and defend a change in the system of production and consumption, a cultural change quite sharp and differentiated from the predatory culture we have now, which would guarantee not only the balance between society and nature but also some kind of balance that would bet on the dignity of all living beings. This, either from the point of view of anthropocentrism or from an alternative point of view.

These four possible scenarios—volitional optimism, ecofascism, collective euthanasia, and the new paradigm—are, as can be derived from their understanding, antagonistic. Here we support the last scenario: the NEP. Something must change so that our relationship with the environment is a fully human, fruitful relationship that does not condition the life on the planet of future generations when it comes to discerning how their existence is configured. To identify the main proposals or hypotheses of this new ecological paradigm, it will be interesting to discern them from the point of view of economics.

The optics that now appear more viable and are academically assumed to understand the current system and see if it is possible and viable to replace it are: the optics of neoliberal capitalism, the optics of green capitalism, and the optics of ecological economy. *Neoliberal capitalism*, broadly speaking, emphasizes that technological substitution is the dominant economic phenomenon. When something is exhausted, something replaces it and nothing happens. When a technology proves to be unhealthy or inconvenient, it is replaced. Up to now, we have functioned in this way. What prevents us from thinking that we can continue to function in this way for ever and ever, if we continue to think and advance in scientific research and development?

Neoliberal capitalism, likewise, understands human knowledge as a resource and affirms that it is inexhaustible. If this resource is present on the planet, there is nothing to fear. They also consider that sustained economic growth guarantees that human knowledge will indeed be able to solve all the problems that arise to guarantee the defense and preservation of the environment. Neoliberal capitalism, as can be inferred, seems to us inadequate, unsustainable, and, to a certain extent, irrational; to propose it as an intellectual proposal that would be useful to understand the environmental problems and the viability of the present system of production and consumption. Its tacit end of the history of optimistic diagnosis is merely volitional.

As an alternative to neoliberal capitalism, *green capitalism* advocates that the market and private initiative be considered and contemplated as decontaminating agents. It also advocates that product prices should include all externalities as well as the regenerative cost deriving from the product production process. And finally, it says that governments should provide fiscal incentives for prices to include the externality and the regenerative cost while refraining from intervening directly in the market and in the economy.

The issue that we believe is particularly interesting and defensible from the point of view of green capitalism (and that we must assume) is that of including externalities and regenerative cost in prices, as we have already mentioned throughout the text. The market does not do it right now, but it could do it if the powers that be make sure that prices represent the true cost—that is, the cleaning of garbage, fumes, and everything that the production process of a given product releases into nature or the environment. The proposal of green capitalism is a proposal that acts from the political power over the economy, and that would guarantee that the market is a viable mechanism to safeguard the environment.

And a third perspective, a third vision, is what we call *ecological economics*. There are two authors who have shaped it: a Romanian, Nicholas Georgescu-Roegen, and an American, Herman Daly, although many other authors have contributed in later developments. For them, economic growth has limits. What the neoliberal capitalists used to say—that sustained economic growth is possible—is unfeasible for those who defend this proposal. Here they advocate the solution of what they call steady state economics: an economy that contemplates development without growth. This implies understanding development in a radically different way from the way it is understood today.

The configuration of a new ecologically viable proposal based on the NEP would have to take from any of the three visions we have mentioned what it considers necessary and healthy for the preservation of the environment. We have already pointed out that from the proposal of neoliberal capitalism practically nothing, from the proposal of green capitalism the price policy, and from the proposal of the ecological economy the steady state economy, seem to us possible and viable. This is where economics must come forward and get involved without delay, because the inertias enshrined in the discipline do not bode well. Virtually all Nobel Prize winners in economics over the last twenty-five years or so, with very few exceptions, have limped on the same leg: they are neoliberal orthodox. This is a trend that, in the opinion of yours truly, must be reversed.

There are four points related to the viability of the NEP with which we could conclude the chapter. Faced with volitional optimism (nothing is happening here and there is no need to worry too much), ecofascism (too much is happening here), or collective euthanasia (this cannot be fixed), we must remember, first, that economic science is a valuative science and therefore normative rather than positive. This is one of the conclusions drawn from the work of two distinguished socioeconomists, Amartya Sen and Amitai

Etzioni, who argue that economic studies should cease reformulating concepts that have been too lightly used up to now before deepening in the matter. Thus, the concepts of value, wealth, and rationality, among others. Economics is a value science: it should not focus on profit maximization mechanisms but on formulating operative concepts that serve to develop viable and ecologically healthy proposals.

Secondly, both economists and sociologists should bear in mind that we must be very careful when measuring populations. Population (a subject that will be dealt with in a separate chapter) is a differentiated whole that we cannot see as a danger to the environment. It is not because it has been measured incorrectly, without differentiating quantity from quality. It is not a question of how many of us there are, but of who are the good and who are the bad, and of proposing that the bad ones stop doing bad things and that the good ones teach the others to do good things. It is not the same, from an environmental point of view, to be born in a country that does not pollute as in another that does. The population, as a differentiated whole, demands more sophisticated measurements to provide the competent bodies with data with which they can operate healthily.

Thirdly, the NEP would remind us that when measuring wealth, we must take into account the meter with which we operate. It has always been said that we measure what matters to the measurer. In my modest opinion, what is really important when measuring wealth is neither the gross domestic product nor the gross national product; wealth should be measured in a different way, taking into account intangible goods and common goods. Only by measuring wealth in a way that takes these goods into account will we be able to define the concept of good and then implement policies of economic growth or degrowth that are healthy, sustainable, and compatible with human development.

Fourth, there is the issue of globalization. Economic globalization and the accompanying rush that it has brought has resulted in a decline in quality. We have suffered a downward leveling, so it is important that when it comes to contemplating, measuring, and rationalizing economic activity, we follow Schumacher's advice and reduce the scales by betting more on localization than on globalization.

The capitalist world system, from an environmental point of view, is a dismal failure. World corporations and global monopolies must come to an end. This protagonism of money, which runs wild throughout the world and which, in some way, is configured as a more important subject than people themselves, is an unworthy protagonism. The globalization of dignity must be understood to constrain economic globalization. In short, we are committed to moving from the logic of the market to the logic of life.

It is a matter of taking life out of the market, taking ecology out, nature out, human beings out: this cannot be traded. We are betting, as we have mentioned, on moving from a politics of representation, that politics that shapes power from the bottom up through which those at the bottom give power to those at the top so that those at the top can act, to one of recuperation of power that goes from the top down, that power is disseminated in society. Some call it empowerment, disseminating power downwards so that responsibility is close and near to the one who executes the action. This, however, is neither more nor less than what has always been called subsidiarity.

We must remember, and with this we end the chapter, that ecologism is a humanism. Ecology should not be understood as something opposed to anthropology. We defend the anthropic principle by considering human subjects as gardeners of nature. This underlines human dignity, and it is unworthy for man to destroy nature and to make the future of life on the planet unviable with the atomic threat. The new ecological paradigm configured around the basic perspectives that we have enunciated, we believe that it configures a future scenario that can be presented as an alternative to other cosmovisions, and we hope that in the academy this proposal will bear fruit in research and specific works that will come to configure a culture of life at a global level. This would indeed be a good globalization.

15. Youth

YOUTH OR YOUNG PEOPLE: subject or object? We will reflect on this, assuming that young people reflect the failures of adults: the needs that have not been satisfied and the virtues that have not been embodied by their elders. The so-called youth crisis is a work in progress in which adults must join with young people to make sense of a common future in which the present plays its part.

In sociology it seems to be unclear whether youth exist. In the social sciences, who we are takes precedence over who I am. We are not an aggregate of selves, but each one is a part of the whole. The social comes before the individual. From the biological point of view, it is like this: we are someone mediating a relationship, and then we are born and survive to the extent that at least the mother-child social relationship works. And from the conceptual point of view as well, because the most radical thing that each one of us is is a daughter or a son, and being a sibling implies a social relationship. But having said this, we will refer to whether youth is an object or a subject: whether it is an object of study that has been fabricated by those who want to study youth, as redheads or fishermen can be an object of study, or whether, on the contrary, youth is not an object. Then we would presuppose that, perhaps, it is a subject, although this is not entirely clear.

A subject can be passive or active. In this case, the choice would be between a passive reproduced subject and an active subject that would be a social subject insofar as it is an original subject. According to almost all those who have studied youth from the point of view of sociology, we would accept that youth is a subject reproduced, replicated, or fabricated for the needs of analysis.

Thus, Pierre Bourdieu's school says that youth is a product and that what exists are young people. A self-perceived product that has its liturgies as rites of passage that focus on sex, violence, and addictions, and then goes from being a product to a process of social transition, in which before there was a unilinear line of transition, which went from an original family to another stable family already in adulthood, and now is a random and uncertain open process with false exits. This is also, with the addition of certain nuances, the position of the Spanish sociologist Gil Calvo, who speaks of youth as a collateral by-product that is alien to the will of its members and therefore cannot be studied by means of surveys. Its members do not construct youth, but youth is reproduced, constructed, by those who pay attention to it.

Many authors have studied youth, and what we are going to say below is not original, but I do not wish to distance myself from several of my colleagues' interpretations. We are going to deconstruct youth to understand it in the sense of deciphering it, not in the sense of destroying it. If we understand youth as a reproduced subject, we ask ourselves who produces that subject. We focus here on the idea that youth and the problems and considerations that affect it refer directly to adult life. It is we adults who cause the problems in youth, who put youth as a reproduced and observable subject, to remove part of a guilt, to remove part of a responsibility. At least in our time, in today's culture, the crisis of youth is, in my opinion, the crisis of adulthood. Where the adult disease hurts are in youth.

The problem, if there is a problem that can be called a problem of youth, is the problem of the habits of adulthood: that which we adults owe to youth and are not giving to them. What are the deficiencies that our passivity produces in our children? That is the question that we should, in my opinion, ask ourselves, and, reflecting on this, I think that there are three aspects that we should focus on. In the first place, exemplarity, along the lines of Javier Gomá's treatment of this issue. We are not being exemplary. We are not providing attractive, true, coherent, exciting, and fulfilling roles.

There is a lack of exemplarity on our part and, consequently, there is also a lack, secondly, of credibility. Credibility has a lot to do with security. If there is one thing adults have to give to young people, it is a perspective of the future. A collective desire to improve a beloved inheritance: an *I want to be like you* and I want, not only to be like you, but, if I can, better than you. And this hopeful credibility has a lot to do with what was said before that the fulfillment of the human being depends on authenticity. To see if we adults are authentic enough to be credible to those who are not yet adults. Here I think we are failing.

And there is also the issue, in third place, of proximity. We are not close enough and therefore we are absent too much. Our close presence can do something good for the youth. The lack of exemplarity, credibility, and proximity takes its toll on our children.

Having said that, we must ask ourselves how we see young people: as a burden, as a curiosity, as those who see parenthood as a biological curiosity, as an insurance? It is sadder if I think that I am going to take care of one or two so that they can take care of me, which is to see young people as a consumer product of ours, a commodity. We can also see them as an affective need in the style of a gifted pet that can replicate caresses. There is a very interesting issue here, which is now being studied, highlighting the contributions of the Israeli sociologist Eva Illouz, who talks a lot about emo-consumption. Perhaps we are thinking not of a youth for itself but a youth for myself, something very typical of the selfishness that undermines credibility in adulthood. When we think of a youth for themselves, for them, perhaps we begin to realize those deficiencies that we must cover so that our children can be for themselves.

It is possible that we are seeing them as the failure of our vital experience and we are condemning them, telling them more or less this: I consider myself a failure; I did not know how to overcome such obstacles, you will not be able to do it either and I will not pass the experience of my failure to you because to pass it to you I would have to overcome that failure. I am referring to the subject of freedom. It happened at the end of the last century, with the great crisis of freedom and, particularly, the problem of the limits of freedom. The aspiration for freedom that ended the twentieth century was about conquering something that supposedly had no limits. We thought that freedom was the erasure of limits. But a freedom without limits is inconceivable, because where there is no limit there is nothing to distinguish freedom from non-freedom. There has to be a limit to distinguish one freedom from another, and the limit, in my opinion, has to do also with hierarchy, in the sense that there are freedoms more important than others. Here we fail in a sea of undifferentiated relativism and subjectivism. Our transition to adulthood resulted, in many people, in a return to intellectual infancy: an immature not-knowing. The after-effects of this misunderstanding are still haunting us with various syndromes, such as the Peter Pan syndrome, the absent male, bigorexia, and others. A series of problems, in short, social problems, which are caused precisely by the failure of many adults to reconcile freedom with its limits.

We were given political freedoms and we thought that all the goods of the earth were at our disposal effortlessly. And those who do not know how to manage their freedom, those who deep down find themselves slaves of materialism or consumerism to the point of addictive behavior, have no recipe for giving instructions to anyone on how to manage their freedom. Because the moment you give him a recipe, that person will ask you: "Hey, why don't you apply it to yourself. I don't believe you."

What young people need and specifically what they need from us is the same as what we need to make our world a fairer world, a world in which diachrony, the passing or succession of generations, operates as a social mechanism that generates wellbeing over time. Therein lies the communication of knowledge, the transmission of knowledge and experiences, and exemplary care. To this effect, we will conclude with three proposals, which are, in our opinion, the needs that we must first try to satisfy for an effective diachrony to operate.

In the first place, commitment. Young people need commitment, and we also need commitment. Commitment has a lot to do with loyalty and constancy. Here we point out one of the great problems of the contemporary world, which is very present when studying youth, and that is inconstancy. Something that is facilitated right now by the addiction to screens that causes a certain impossibility to deepen knowledge. Moving from one thing to another, changing quickly, generates inconstancy, and this is cured with commitment. Loyalty with perseverance affects all aspects of social life, friendship, or marriage itself for example. That there are so many divorces today is because, among other reasons, we need to understand better what we call commitment, that we value loyalty more, that inconstancy seems to us a defect and a disposable vice.

The second need is trust. The hopelessness that our world is experiencing and that is in the air requires that we cover it with trust. Trust has a lot to do with freedom. If we use freedom well, it will give us confidence. It will also give us resources and responsiveness, a power that is self-mastery and that many people now lack because they are very comfortable being dominated, being protected. Because one is satisfied with the choices that one is given, without looking for more alternatives or choosing the opposite. Trust is born within us and is a consequence of the good use of freedom.

And thirdly, we must also give them reasons. Some literature has rightly contrasted reasons with emotions, and we are in a culture dominated by emotions. The aspiration to be reasonable is, however, unrenounceable. It is satisfied with study, learning, and wisdom. If we could show the state and shortcomings of our world by accusing ourselves of having made it this way, if we were capable of showing the young people these shortcomings by asking forgiveness for them, we would feed the necessary rebellion that must take place in the youth of today in order to change the world. And in this process, we, the adults, should join them.

It is up to us to be the revolutionaries we were not before and, in some way, to trust. There is an author I like very much, with a fantastic book titled *The Power of the Powerless*. It is Vaclav Hável who advises us to fight in small aspects that have to do with our life, with our virtues, with our attitudes, with the recognition of our shortcomings, to discover ourselves hopeful (to change the world). It is about fighting to be able to be exemplary, to be able to give credibility, and to be able to approach that youth, which we now contemplate from afar and which is nothing more than the epigone of our failures.

16. The Profession

THE PROFESSION IS OUR labor identity. Professions are at odds with the instrumental vision of work and, like work, are fulfilling and have intrinsic value. The decline of the profession in our time is temporary and awaits the birth of an economy open to plural utilities in societies with more and better organic solidarity.

It is said that the professions are in the doldrums. It is not a situation that we think will last forever. It is a temporary decline due to the crisis of the end of modernity in which we are immersed. It should be noted that we are referring to the profession as an identity, a peculiar identity similar to what we mean when we say that someone professes. Profession, like professing, derives from doing. It is usually said that first it is the being and then the doing; well, the profession is a being that does, and this doing feeds back to the being to form a precise identity: it is what we are. In the past, in the national identity documents, the profession was also included. The profession is something that, even if we do not practice it, identifies us as what we are. It is a source of personal fulfillment and has a social mission.

We perform our profession in front of others, something that can even be socially visible. In the past, professions were shown in clothing, just as other identities are denoted. There is men's fashion and there is women's fashion if we refer to sexual identity, and there are also uniforms specific to professions. Today, in this decline of professions, it seems that the only uniform that remains is the military uniform, but if we review history, we see that there were uniforms for almost all professions. Even today, a uniform that almost all of us wear is the ring that denotes our identity as people who are married or not. The visibility of the profession denotes its social function. Thus, a person has a profession and exercises it, regardless of whether that profession is identified with a job. We can thus speak of a full profession and a passive profession. A full profession would be the ordinary exercise of work subject to a regime, and a passive profession would be that same person when he is on working vacation, when he is resting, when he is on sick leave, when he is unemployed, or when he retires.

The profession, insofar as it is our labor identity, necessarily refers to work, and one of the causes of this temporary decline of the profession derives from the very concept of work. There is great confusion about what it is to work, what it is to work for, what the purpose of work is, or what orientation we give to work. These are issues that have been central to the sociology of work and still are. Sociology has often defined employment as paid work. But this is not quite so. There are remunerations that do not imply work, for example unemployment benefits, and there are jobs that are not remunerated, for example domestic work. Work should not be confused with employment. A profession is the exercise of a specific job, but work is the result of a social construction. It is a form of expansion of the self as a service together with love, together with care, together with belonging: different ways of expressing a person's identity.

In the past, there was this distinction between work that was considered good or positive, and work that was considered bad or negative. In former times, when one dedicated oneself to the exercise of arms, or when one entered religion, when one lived on income, when one worked in one's house, in the *domus*, when one dedicated oneself to the arts or to letters, one was doing a positive thing. And yet they were considered pejorative jobs, servile jobs, menial or forced labor, or that of the slave. In our time there is one error of that history that survives with us, and that is to understand work as utility, as something that can be introduced in the market to buy and sell.

Hence the pejorative approach that, many times, from the business point of view, is given to human labor as something undesirable. Labor would be an undesirable utility insofar as the more work machines can do instead of humans, the cheaper the product will be and therefore the better it will be for the company. This is a serious mistake. Work is not a utility. Rather, it is the other way around: work should not be set aside because work is something identifying and fulfilling through the profession. Work is not just another factor of production. Work is considered an end, not a means; it is not a product.

This is not clear to many of those who dedicate themselves to economic science. To understand work as what it is, with a finalist conception, as something that is intrinsically human and that belongs to the identity of each person and that, therefore, is necessary for personal fulfillment, is closely linked to the concept of profession. Let us try to explain the decline of the professions in the contemporary world. What has happened so that the professions, nowadays, are almost not contemplated in real life, so that they are not visible, so that they are not seen, so that one does not identify oneself with one's profession. We see here a set of several causes.

The first is the confusion in the relationship between work and leisure: if work is something instrumental, or if work is something fulfilling. If work is instrumental, then one works to fulfill oneself in leisure. If work is something fulfilling, one, on the contrary, rests in leisure to fulfill oneself in work. According to the whole sociological tradition, to the classics and to the current leaders of the discipline, work is something fundamental in society and, therefore, work must be fulfilling. To consider work as instrumental is to denigrate not only work and the profession but the human condition itself.

Another cause, which we could point out when it comes to understanding this decline of the profession, is materialism. The primacy of money confuses work with salary, confusing the aspiration to fulfill oneself as a professional with the aspiration to fulfill oneself by spending or earning money. We are in an era in which consumer materialism prevails, in which having is more important than, not only being, but even doing. This primacy of money, this focus only on salaries and prices, is something that has been and continues to be in opposition to the fulfilling and identifying aspect of professions and work itself.

We can see a new cause in the rise of technology. Technology has decreased specialization and has replaced many jobs. Robotics has put on the horizon that theme, to which several books have already been dedicated, which is the end of human work. They wonder what a life without work will be like. That is impossible. There may be a life without employment, but a life without work is no life. The human being is fulfilled by working; it is a different thing whether he earns a salary or not. That is why work, as we will see later, is something that can imply a counterpart of satisfaction, which will be through a salary, but which can also be mediated through free work, which is part of what has been called the gift economy.

Technology, and particularly robotics, is making many people change jobs. The profession can be changed, but it is something, an identifying mark of one's identity, which when changed produces, in many cases, an important personal crisis. One must be very careful, because to change profession many times is to stop being what one is to be something else. It can be done, but it is difficult, and technology is forcing us in certain professions to make these changes, and in an unexpected way. What a sad thing, it is the same sadness that the Luddites referred to in the years 1820 to 1830 when Luddism in Great Britain and in some other parts of the world jumped to the forefront of public interest, like those people who, to defend their jobs, went against the machines and destroyed the looms in the manufacture of cloth. Technology is not going to such extremes today, but there are many people who feel cheated because they lose their jobs—mostly in service companies. I am thinking right now about what happened recently in banking. You used to go to the bank to do business and you would find a person, with a friendly face, but with whom you could communicate. Now you go there, and you have a machine, and then you wonder what has happened, where is that person now, because maybe they have lost their job or have been early retired, and it is not something that person could have chosen. How are they going to present themselves in society now? The irruption of technology without preparation in, what is now called with a terminology that I do not like, the labor market, is producing perverse effects because the transition has been made very badly and for spurious purposes.

And finally, another cause to be highlighted is the conception of the public sphere as something neutral and secular, resulting in the invisibilities of the people who make the public what it is, a space to be dwelt. Apart from the loss of presence of professional identity signs (uniforms) or personal signs of belonging, a generalized aesthetics of power and submission is consolidated, reducing the plurality of the public space in the understanding that what is plural is not neutral. No, there is no such thing as a neutral identity. Socially, as well as personally, we also have identities, and public environments should reflect these diversities. If everything public were neutral in this sense throughout the world, there would be no visible human diversity. If we relegate identities to the private sphere, if we cannot express them, we are nobody. Identity is expressive, otherwise it is not identity. The conception of the public, as something uniform and neutral, is detrimental to any human fulfillment, including also that identity we are calling profession.

The finalistic conception of work and profession has much to do with the theory of value. Here Durkheim's contribution is capital. I assume that there are four orientations to working: instrumental, bureaucratic, transcendent, and solidarity. I refer here to the last two.

We are seeing that both work and profession have a meta-economic character, that their purpose is intrinsic to the fact of developing that work and that profession. Their valuation, the importance given to them, in the context in which they operate, determines cultures, as well as collective identities. The theory of value is a subject studied in sociology and economics, and is, in my opinion, a determining factor when it comes to proposing an economy with meaning, a realization through work, and an identitarian profession.

To this effect, we can mention the classical theory of value, which identifies the value of things with work, both in quantity and quality: what has been invested to develop a given product. Famous figures such as Adam

Smith, Robert Owen, William Godwin, and David Ricardo militated in this classical theory of value. The so-called classical theory of value had little trajectory because soon, with liberalism, came the still prevailing neoclassical theory. For the neoclassical theory, the value of products—and even, for many, the value of labor and human beings—is determined by market opportunity, by supply and demand. Here, it is said that the classic Castilian writer Francisco Quevedo said in the seventeenth century, "*es de necios confundir valor con precio*" (it is foolish to confuse value with price).

Among the founding fathers, so called, of sociology, this subject has been treated in depth. Marx has an approach to the theory of value dealing with the problem of price: how can prices be fixed in a fair way without those prices being subject to the law of supply and demand, without labor being involved in the market, and without the market encompassing everything? Marx invents this figure of accumulated labor and then, to give the value of things, there would be direct labor and indirect labor or accumulated labor, which becomes a zero-sum set that makes up the cooperative spirit, land, and capital. It is very difficult to specify what Marx really thought about value, but he takes a step forward to distinguish price from value starting from the profound critique he makes of capitalism.

For Durkheim, the organic functionality of the productive process, and of a whole society, is what gives value to things. Here, it is not only important to have whatever product it is in which labor and resources have been invested, but it is important to know how it has been produced, by whom, where, etc., and that will give value as well. It is something very modern, especially now with the ecological concern. A product, if it has been developed with certain scarce resources or not, if it is ecological, if it is environmentally healthy, if it has perverse additives, it will have one value or another. The value is given, not only by the product itself, but by circumstances in which the purpose of the work that has been put into the elaboration of the product and how that purpose has been made operative are taken into account.

And then there is Max Weber, for whom ethics and values count, because here we will also have not only an evaluation of things and of the product, but also an evaluation of the culture and of the society in which that product becomes present and useful. Here the environment, religion, and culture, to the extent that the productive and commercial process participates in them, form a pathos that gives a finalist and transcendent sense to work and, as a consequence, gives a peculiar value to attitudes, aptitudes, and labor and commercial uses.

We see that the theory of value determines the different approaches to human labor. The value marks meaning when talking about work and profession. With all that has been said, it is convenient to underline Durkheim's contribution in a book, in my opinion seminal, *On the Division of Social Labor* of 1893, in which he points out the relationship between the division of labor and organic solidarity. Specifically, Durkheim's view is that in the professions, insofar as they operate in the public sphere, they enmesh society. If I take care of this and I know you take care of that and I know you're going to do it well, then I take care of mine and you take care of yours and we benefit society as a whole. It is a very nice idea, and, in my opinion, it deserves to be rescued in order to understand what professions are, and what they should be in the future.

The neoclassical contribution of the theory of value, as we have already mentioned, did a lot of damage to the profession, but we ought to mention the history of trade unionism also did a lot of damage. Curiously, because when the working day is introduced and the working day is measured in time, in a way, what is said is that what the worker sells when receiving a salary is his time. It is something, we could say, akin to slavery: I become a slave for hours, I give my time, I give myself for a period of time, and in exchange I receive a salary. This is not professional. It is not at all fair and it is perfectly understandable that Durkheim spoke to us of anomie and that Marx spoke to us of alienation as the likely result of this exchange. The history of trade unionism, in this sense, has not been good for the defense of the professions when it comes to equating everyone in what we can call the sale of time. What we sell is not time; if anything we sell products that we have produced for a time, and that, in a way, are ours because what gives value to these products is, ultimately, our work. Thus, it is taken into account who has made them, who has manufactured them, where, how, when, etc.

There are two unionist traditions, the Anglo-Saxon unionist tradition and the continental one, we could say. The Anglo-Saxon tradition has tried to defend the professions, and that has been frankly positive until quite recently. Now, perhaps not so much, when the differences have blurred and what unionism tries to defend is the salary and not the profession. Then the results become, as far as the work and the profession are concerned, quite defective.

The contribution that a profession makes to society is very important and if what is being defended is my salary, the message we give is that what makes me happy is money. All this calls the economy to rethink certain things, and in the first place, to rethink mono-utility: that of thinking that the objective of the economy is to maximize profit, that the only utility that counts, at the end of the day, is profit. That I invest my labor in the company always seeking the same thing, the maximization of profit, is patently false, and this was already demonstrated by Amitai Etzioni when he wrote *The*

Moral Dimension, confirming that altruism was perfectly rational and that there were other utilities that should be considered. We have discussed this in *Socioeconomía* (1997) or *Socioeconomics*, where we advocate the previously mentioned dematerialization.

We should contemplate the infinite resources of the service, and that the process of production and consumption does not close with the sale of the product or with the warranty period but closes by also incorporating the externality. The economy should rectify its conception of the subject in order not to understand us exclusively as producers or exclusively as consumers, but as people who realize themselves through their work, in the exercise of their profession.

The defect of economic individualism clashes here with an alternative proposal of corporatist type, to see in the social reality the protagonism of corporations, professional associations, and trade unions in their Anglo-Saxon version. I see the need for these collectives, which are concerned with defending professions and their improvement, in order not to have isolated individuals who confront powerful companies or who are only consumers. If we consider that those who consume are individuals in a market that is, and this is the last point we wanted to emphasize, all-encompassing, then the market would have room for everything. And no, there are "products" that should not be offered in the market, such as, in my opinion, human time, or those identity variables that define and characterize each one of us.

There is an underlying theme in all this, and that is job orientation. In sociology of work texts, four main orientations are usually studied. There is the instrumental orientation, the bureaucratic orientation, the solidarity orientation, and the transcendent orientation. The instrumental orientation is the one linked to wages, the bureaucratic orientation is linked to security, the solidarity orientation is linked to civility, and the transcendent orientation is linked to morality. And it is a pity that most of the current work orientations are the first two. The instrumental orientation sees work as an instrument for earning a salary, while the bureaucratic orientation sees it as a mechanism to ensure security within the framework of a welfare or protective state.

The other two orientations, solidarity and transcendence, are unfortunately underrepresented in the surveys. And it would be desirable for them to be much more so, given their social and cultural repercussions. There are types of labor organizations that do promote them. Thus, solidarity is present, at least in theory, in cooperative enterprises. However, the transcendent orientation, which is very important and real at the same time, because the whole economy of gift and the economy of gratuity have in their design a

transcendent starting point, is sometimes not even mentioned in the manu-
als. What a mistake!

To conclude this chapter, I should remind you of something that is of
great concern to this writer, and that is the issue of plurality. Plurality is a
consequence of the exercise of freedom (where there is no plurality there is
no freedom) and the professions give us identity plurality. They differentiate
us and it is good that they differentiate us. Now that there is so much talk
about herd immunity, it is good that we do not see our work identities as
herd identities. We professionals complement each other and see ourselves
as those sails on a sailboat that are on different masts but all contribute to
the wind propelling the ship. Thus, the professions drive society, safeguard
our jobs, ensure our plural identities, and, with them, it is good that we once
again consider ourselves as people who fulfill ourselves by working, giving a
meta-economic and non-instrumental character to our work.

Rethinking and defending the professions, as well as inventing all
those needed for this new era that is opening up, is a matter of paramount
importance. It is important that we return to considering the professions as
something fulfilling, as an exciting goal for every human being. Let us aim,
then, for economic science, economic programs, to contemplate the non-
cash economy, the economy of intangible goods, the immaterial economy,
and the purposes of productive exercise and commercial activity, as well as
the subjects who, through their professional identities, interact with each
other. Something without which, in our modest opinion, we will be able to
assure neither freedom nor self-mastery in the time to come.

17. Health

THERE ARE THREE MAIN domains of health that, as a whole, comprise a new understanding for an accurate comprehension of life. And their distinction and understanding will be very useful for the time to come.

This is, in a way, a post-pandemic reflection, dealing with the concept of social health that I have been working on for years. It is a particularly appealing concept for me because, in the now distant doctoral thesis, the authors I studied, several of whom could be said to be anarchists, used to dismiss their letters with the word "health." I remember that in my childhood I was amazed when my elders, when saying goodbye to each other, used to say "God give you health" or "May the Lord preserve our health" and I, who was a little boy, was astonished at how important health must have been for them, unlike for me. At that age, I thought there were more important things. Now, as the years have gone by, I do think that health is very, very important. But not health understood only as the absence of disease, but in a much broader sense.

The three dimensions of health to which we are going to refer are: the domain of intimacy, the domain of extimacy, and the domain of collectivity. The domain, in the sense of state, of intimacy is health from the point of view of our intimate or individual self, and here we can visualize three main subdomains, which are physical health, psychic health, and spiritual health. In short, these are the subdomains in which we can predicate the health of that compound of soul and body that each one of us is. Physical health is what people mostly understand as the absence of disease, something that doctors treat, or try to treat, more or less fortunately. In psychic health, medicine also has a role to play, but other fields such as psychology intervene. We understand spiritual health, in a broad sense, as tranquility of conscience, as a healthy relationship with the divinity that forms healthy environments in which virtues and values are proposed.

Not necessarily all of this must come from our intimacy outwards,
thus, in the domain of intimacy health, we pursue a healthy, balanced personality, which is at the same time kind and happy, and that leads us to
speak of that harmonious set of physical, psychic, and spiritual health. This
harmony is necessary for a person to start from a premise of happiness and
aspire to a goal of human fulfillment.

In the second domain, that of extimacy, we refer both to the empty-
ing of extimacy that we observe in social networks, and to the exchange of
extimacy that we call relationship. Here we can situate two main subdomains: family health and relational health. Family health aims at functional
optimums in the fulfillment of the functions that society expects from it.
The most important social subject is the family, and we are human because
we are family members, as has already been made clear. We have extimacy
because we have been the fruit of extimacy. All humans are, as we have
repeated, daughters or sons, and therein lies our most basic radicality. Family health refers to the home environment in which one is not only born,
but also lives, forming a collective individuality that we call family. Family
health is measured with love and this has consequences that can be counted
in terms of mutual support, trust, devotion, service, and care.

On the other hand, the subdomain of relational health is that exchange
of intimacies that make up the relational extimacy, which is not as deep
as in the family, but which makes up other types of subjects of friendship,
neighborhood communities, extended family communities, age communities, religious communities, etc. All that nourishes, vivifies, and makes these
communities function is their health. In relational health there are two very
interesting aspects, and usually neglected, and that is that extimacy and intimacy feed back to the extent that spiritual health affects family health, and
physical and psychological health affect relational health, while these two,
family health and relational health, also have to do with spiritual health,
physical health, and psychological health. The border created by extimacy
is positive because it places us in reality, here we have called it strangeness.
Thus, family health and relational health can also deteriorate through ex-
cesses that ignore strangeness.

The third domain is that of collectivity, of everyone. If that of intimacy
was the self and that of extimacy was the we, that of collectivity is the all.
Here too there are subdomains: social health, public health, and corporate
health. Social health is something we measure from the point of view of the
quality of our relationships. Thus, for example, freedom, peace, or equity,
values on which the social health of a recognized everyone depends. There
are different methods of measurement and various contributions have been
made, such as those studied and proposed in the work *La Salud Social*

(1999). Public health handles more quantitative concepts of health and adds to social health the component of verticality since government action has a great predicament there. We are referring to food health, environmental health, security, or education. Something that comes from a culture of governance or positive self-governance. Public health is not only what is studied and practiced by those engaged in the practice of this medical subdiscipline, but also and fundamentally social and political aspects that have an impact on well-being. Finally, corporate, or organizational health, focuses on occupational health, the health of companies, churches, and the various corporations that are present in almost all societies and that make up some kind of collective identity.

We have gone from a concept of health, which is the one commonly used in language, which is restrictive and primarily medical, to a much broader concept. Intimacy, extimacy, and collectivity are the referential spheres of progress, happiness, or fulfillment. We realize ourselves individually, in groups and globally and, increasingly, we also realize ourselves in geographical terms on a planetary scale, and we cannot embrace this planetary terminology without broadening the concept of health. We are all concerned with health because it is something very broad that affects several undertakings and functionalities at the same time. It is such a complex and vast subject that it implies a necessary division of intellectual labor to be able to cover it with a minimum of rationality.

Perhaps, of all the subdomains of health that we have mentioned, social health, public health, family health, and spiritual health are the ones that require the most in-depth study and research, because they are the least known, not only among the general public but also among experts. Thus, in the academy, in the university, in research, and in intellectual work in general, we should deepen and broaden the concept, so that it reaches the political decision-making bodies with a transforming impulse. In short, we believe that if there is anything that justifies politics, it is health understood in this way, and we also believe that this is where true and genuine equality resides. Politics, it seems, has much to do with hygiene, asepsis, and the purification of pathogenic elements.

18. Generation and Degeneration

As a STARTING POINT in this chapter, we focus on the generative fact that discovers us as dependent children. A moment in which biology implies sociology, and which encapsulates the human being as a family being based on filiation. The subject is capital to glimpse a viable future.

For what will come after modernity, if anything, when speaking of generation and degeneration, we will start from solid assumptions. In the first place, that we human beings are social beings before being individuals; in the end, we become conscious individuals because we have been socialized in properly human relationships. And, secondly, that what is radically human, what sustains us as humanity, if we had to refer everything to a condition, is filiation. We have already dealt with this in other chapters, but here we will start from it to speak of birth and death.

We are moral subjects in a double sense: in the sense that each of us is a moral subject, and in the sense that each of us participates in many other moral subjects. The communities in which we participate and to which we belong are always being shaped as moral subjects. Humanity, we can say, is a process and not a state, beyond the point of departure, which is where we are going to focus first. We have already underlined filiation and, going a little deeper, we realize that, contrary to paternity or responsibility, it is something that we, none of us, has chosen. By the filiation we are given, also, the fraternity and other relations and innate familiar bonds.

Speaking of the types of filiations, we can speak of a genetic filiation, which can be modified or not modified, manipulated or not manipulated, and which some call chromosomal filiation. We can also speak of an affective-familial filiation, or of another, of a legal-cultural type. The important thing is to understand filiation as this immediate or proximate transgenerational relationship, and by delving there, we realize that there is an intrinsic and important relationship between two branches of knowledge: biology and sociology. Seeing our filial condition from biology, we point out that this necessarily implies sociology, because the relationships that make up the family are what ultimately make us human. Human biology points us to a differential factor, which is social dependence: we are dependent beyond breastfeeding. When breastfeeding ends, we continue to be dependent, to the point that we cannot survive without this basic social relationship. In order to become human, we need the social.

We may ask ourselves how is it that evolution, if we can speak of evolution here, has not taken care of this and "liberated" us from this relational dependence. We think that it has not freed us, because this social dependence is constitutively essential, and if it is essential then we are doomed to the study of our family condition. This is, as they say, the crux of the matter. We humans, as we have said before, are radically familiar and it is good to underline and repeat this because we usually do not realize it.

It is really serious that in the academy there is no perception that we are radically familiar starting from our filial condition. For that reason, the family has been studied little, and when it has been done, it has been focused on the family in solitary and not from the point of view of the economy or the law as a subject with its own and differentiated personality. If we were to study the family as the subject that solves this problem of dependence, we would immediately realize that there is an innate family condition from the generative starting point that demands stability.

Stability is a conditioning factor of our identity permanence, and in the need for stability we realize that the family is not a circumstance. When we look back, our life makes sense. In the 2002 film *Thirteen Conversations About One Thing*, directed by Jill Sprecher, the colleague of one of the protagonists, played by Alan Arkin, tells him, in a relaxed moment in a bar, that it is a pity that our life goes forward but that it only makes sense when we look back. Indeed, when we search our history for who we are, family takes on a prominence that it does not take on when we usually look forward. There is a lesson here, and it is that the best policy, the best foresight, is that which fundamentally considers the family reality.

It is in the family reality that what we call human generation is produced. Forgetting this very important issue—the relationship between family, generation, and human future—is very pernicious. Fatal, for that which we have called progress, and which is one of the referent creeds of modernity. Perhaps modernity has ended, precisely because of this: because we have not known how to incorporate the family relationship in our projects for the future. Individualism has grown so rampant that we have forgotten our social condition and, above all, our radical dependence at the beginning of our generation. It is important, therefore, to think broadly in terms of the family.

I have been very critical of the pairing that has been made between marriage and family studies. Many people think that families begin with marriage, and this writer has always said that they do not. The family comes before marriage, and to underline this, as if making a joke and jocularly, I have said that yours truly is against marriage. The students in front of me get a shock saying: how can you say that? And then I explain myself, more or less in this way: I am against anti-family marriage because nowadays the level of confusion is so high that we have put so many possible combinations in the concept of marriage that have blurred it and we are not able to make that capital distinction between family and anti-family marriage. And then one went on to say that there is a marriage that does not ensure stability, or that is not capable of solving the problems of dependency in the generation: the anti-family marriage. That is the marriage that excludes the family, like some of the marriages that open themselves to divorce and not only to separation from the start. I, honestly, do not believe in that marriage. Moreover, it seems to me that it is pernicious to use the same term to speak of anti-family marriages and family marriages, which is why I say that I am in favor of the family over marriage. Here I give precedence to diachrony over synchrony because I think that the basis of the family is not nuptiality, but filiation. Families do not begin with marriage as if we were to begin to be family members there. No, we are family members by birth, we are sons, and we never cease to be so.

What a great mistake the church made, I usually say, by not changing the name of the Christian sacrament when it was mocked by the state. If a state can annul a religious marriage, can divorce a canonical marriage, and thereby destroy a family if that marriage has children and mostly if it has dependent or small children, then that state can do it all. The church did not defend itself from this interference. Moreover, in some countries, not content with that, the church gave the state the monopoly of marriage. This distinction between family and no family marriage must be made to save the family and, therefore, I think that the family is much more important than marriage. The justification for marriage is the family. At the end of the lecture, there was a surprise in the classroom. We talk about the subject and exchange reflections, but I had made clear to them something that, perhaps, we are not used to thinking about, because we are not used to thinking in a family way. Because individualism has so permeated our lives that it is preventing us from doing so.

The family must be put in the first place when talking about human generation. The most important power and self-mastery that we humans have is our own existence. That is, reproduction. And if this power, this self-control, is persecuted in many countries by the state, when it restricts the freedom of generation, then we are in a very bad way. Generation cannot be actively or passively penalized, neither legally nor economically, nor socially, but neither can it be discriminated against. And when it is not subsidized, it is because we have not been able to think in, from, and for the family. The family is not our decision, we are a decision of the family. When the decision is made by conditioning, in such a way that generation remains outside the human sphere, we are doomed to degeneration.

It is important that we think of human generation from assumptions that elevate us from considering ourselves as a merely individual subject to considering ourselves as a family subject. But from the beginning, and this means before the beginning, because our generation has a preterit: the preexisting social relationship between our parents and so on. Hence, one thinks that the harmful thing about divorce is not that it separates the spouses, which is harmful, but the diachronic separation between grandparents and grandchildren. This breaks a line of transmission of humanity, since humanity is not only given by our biological conditionings, but these have a fixed link with social conditionings that we cannot ignore. It is the family, and when speaking of human generation, we must always keep it in mind.

But beyond the healthy interweaving of biology and sociology at the threshold of life, there is another, to which we must pay attention between medicine and sociology at the threshold of death. The family, we said, is a non-state public good, and another public good, of which we have already spoken, is health. Health, in terms of individual health care, is the responsibility of the administrative bodies of each country. And when the administrations interfere in health issues (which is more than medical or clinical health) that affect the family as a subject, as they generally do not know about it, they spread problems.

Focusing on the degeneration, or the possible degeneration that we are living in our time, and which refers to the causes of death, we can ask ourselves about the qualifier "human." When we review history, we realize that everything we think of as inhuman has been practiced, and sometimes practiced many, many times and to unsuspected limits, by us humans. We can even distinguish between those things that we think are perverse like pederasty, for example, those that are unjust like violent attacks, others that can be abominable like a collective slaughter, and we reserve the qualifier of inhuman, as a further degree, to things of which historically we also have experience, such as the exposure of children, slavery, abortion, torture, or cannibalism. How is it that we say that something that humans have practiced, sometimes profusely, is inhumane? Perhaps because we are moving forward, in the sense that throughout history we have accumulated all these experiences, and we are a little more aware of what gives us humans dignity or detracts from it.

We have seen that family and filiation gave us basic dignity. Can we also speak of dignity at the time of death? We start from the fact that sociology has a lot to do with medicine. In fact, these are two sciences that share the same purpose, the same object and the same method, but differ in the place where they operate. Medicine in the human body and sociology in the human group. This intimate relationship between sociology and medicine, between social health and bodily health, converges in some very concrete issues. One of them, particularly important in our time, is suicide. How is it that so many people commit suicide today? Some speak of the hidden plague and, in some so-called developed countries, suicide is the leading cause of death among young people. In fact, one of the great fathers of the discipline, the previously mentioned Émile Durkheim, wrote in 1897 a work that is still valid today, called *Suicide*. There he spoke of different types of suicide: altruistic suicide, egoistic suicide, anomic suicide, and fatalistic suicide.

Durkheim has been a pioneer in many things, and there is something that also affects the subject we are dealing with, which is a distinction he wrote about in the already mentioned *On the Division of Social Labor*, and that is between mechanical solidarity and organic solidarity. The Frenchman said that, in his time, we were moving from a mechanical industrial solidarity in which individuals were homogeneous and shared values and beliefs, to another organic solidarity in which individuals are different, but share a team spirit to perform different functions. Now a reverse process is occurring. We are moving from organic solidarity to mechanical solidarity to the extent that we are becoming replicants of each other, to the extent, too, that many of us are subject to the same powers, and to the extent, finally, that we behave along the same lines and obey the same fashions. Here isolationist individualism makes its presence felt. It seemed that individualism was going to differentiate us, but it has ended up making us uniform. Isolationist individualism has a lot to do with anti-amatory selfishness, and this leads to something that we believe is at the root of the causes of the possible degeneration of our times, which is sexual involution. But let us go by parts.

We have talked about suicide: what is it, what is the cause? If we go to medicine and sociology at the same time, we see that we can distinguish whether the cause of a disease is behavior or contingency. We will need to see if the case of suicide is in its origin caused by a psychosocial type of disease, or by another of a social type, which may be related to the detachment of one from the other. Whenever I have spoken on the subject, I have always referred to an experience that had an impact on me when I was a student, many years ago. The professor told me what happened with that researcher from the golden days of sociology in the US, who, on seeing some statistics from a small town in New York state where people had a long life expectancy, and realizing that this small town was inhabited by people who were descendants of Greek immigrants, initially thought that this notably higher life expectancy was due to the Mediterranean diet. But it was only a hypothesis and so he went to check it out. He did some field work in the village in question and his results were tremendously enlightening. Contrary to what he thought, he found that in other villages where the population also had a Greek origin, there was not such a high life expectancy. He found as a differential factor of the village in question, that the long life expectancy of the place was due to social factors, community support, that the elderly people did not feel lonely, and in fact there were very few elderly people living alone. Here we have an example of how social factors have a direct impact on the socialization defect that affects life expectancy.

Another issue that may draw our attention, and which has to do with the experience of that sociologist's fieldwork in that small town at the beginning of the twentieth century, is how it is that in US statistics, today, the so-called racial group that has the highest life expectancy are Hispanics, the descendants of immigrants from further down the Rio Grande. What has happened for them to have a higher life expectancy than the whites, called Caucasians? It is due to the same thing: the social involvement of Latinos. This is another example of the relationship between sociology and medicine, insofar as we can understand medicine as a weapon that protects life from illness to guarantee bodily or psychological health, while sociology, in turn, does the same for social health.

Earlier we noted the effects of sexual involution (one calls involution what others call revolution), which also has a lot to do with the decrease in life expectancy. When the community (family) spirit, which should accompany us throughout our lives, diminishes, the end of life is less ideal than when the mutual support in which the community lives becomes visible. It is important, therefore, to have a good understanding of sexual involution and its causes and contexts. In my opinion, we can separate three main stages of the so-called sexual revolution. The first occurred at the end of the 1960s, and we label it as the end of sexual love: that separation between sex and reproduction that eventually produces that finality. The second is at the end of the 1980s, when the deviation disappears and denormalization is accepted. And the third, at the end of the 1990s, which we would label as the end of sex, and which is characterized by repro-genetics, which can even produce coital pleasure without the need for sex and human generation without sexual activity. All these changes have produced an important social attrition, insofar as a notable degree of communitarian detachment has been introduced. The detachment that pursues autonomy and independence also produces loneliness and, in the long run, a shortening of life expectancy.

This has to do with medicine and health sciences, whose aim is to prevent disease, cure the sick, ensure individual and, as far as possible, public health. There are two relevant approaches that need to be mentioned now. In medicine today, there is medicine for the rich and medicine for the poor. That of the rich is antecedent medicine, which tries to intervene in the causes that shorten life expectancy so that life is not only longer but also more satisfactory. That of the poor is consequential medicine, which acts after the disease has appeared. Antecedent medicine is found in some medical practices, common today, such as in vitro fertilization, experimentation with embryos, proposals and practices of transgenic and cloning, or aesthetic medicine. Another interesting division, already mentioned, is that between behavioral and contingency diseases. Increasingly, medicine is intervening in behavioral diseases (particularly addictions and lifestyles) that have much to do with the social. We replicate behaviors as people behave in a uniform way in environments where they share not only language, tradition, or culture, but also age or status. Here, the implication between sociology and medicine can shed light on the moment of death.

In the same way as with birth, to study the moment of death one must know how to count it. There is a subject on which I worked at the time and which has been impossible for me so far, and that is the study of life expectancy in a scientific and serious way, defining very well when we begin to count. It is important that we reason about society, health, love, or sex from non-immanentist and transcendent assumptions. We try to transcend the person, from the horizontal point of view, to his or her close sphere of relationships or social sphere. And also, from the vertical point of view to the field of belief. The fundamental issue, when it comes to counting, is when we start to do it. Earlier we said that suicide in some countries is the first cause of death among young people, but this is not quite so, or according to how, because, if we start counting when life begins (and not when birth occurs or twenty-four hours after birth as in some places), the first cause of death is intrauterine: abortion. Yes, I think that we should try to start counting from the beginning of life. If we count victims, which is what we are talking about, from the middle of the twentieth century until now, never before in the history of humanity, and that is where the degeneration is, the line that separates the human and the inhuman has been so blurry. As a result, so many people, we say, had died from causes procured by themselves or by others without that death being attributable to any contingency disease.

They are deaths caused by us (in the case of abortion) or in ourselves (in the case of suicide). The numbers are overwhelming and anyone who delves into it will have no choice but to stop and think about what is happening to us, why we are killing ourselves like this.

Certainly, the value of life today is in question. There is even talk of useful life, of autonomous life, as if the lives of some human groups were worth more than those of other groups. The value of life is not something that is clear in our time, as it was clear in others, and that is why the most important social statistic that exists, both for sociology and for medicine, is when, how, and from what, people die. Hopefully these figures that are now so hard to find, those of suicide and abortion, will come to light, but not only as someone who announces something bad so that it does not spread, but as something normal on the part of those who put their finger on the sore spot to point out what is most important. Here it is, in my modest opinion, the present human degeneration and I dare to say that a degeneration unparalleled in the history of mankind.

19. "To Govern Is to Populate"

THE TITLE IN QUOTATION marks refers to a phrase of obtuse taste of the Argentine politician Juan Bautista Alberdi in his famous *Bases* of 1852. He was referring to populating well, and although for him these implied racist practices, he was not wrong in underlining the link between demography and politics. The connection is obvious, and, for this reason, sociology has been concerned with the study of populations and has given rise to sub-disciplines which, as in the case of the human ecology developed by the Chicago School in the 1920s, deal with the relationship between the population and its immediate physical environment.

In the task of better understanding and comprehending social reality, we sociologists have needed to ask ourselves a series of questions, such as how many inhabitants there are in a given space, at what rate they reproduce, how many leave and how many enter and why, what is their composition by age, sex, or occupation, etc. To face these questions, it is necessary to know demography. However, population can be studied from different perspectives. Nevertheless, academic experience has made us wary of the dangers that "disciplinarism" represents for a better understanding of the human population experience. Specifically, we must refer to two perspectives that have overemphasized their disciplinary peculiarities when studying population. We are talking about economics and population biology.

Attempts to legitimize an "economics of population" are already evident in the work of Malthus and, above all, in his famous *Essay* of 1798, as well as in the population postulates of certain primitive economic schools such as the mercantilists, the physiocrats, and Adam Smith himself. For this "disciplinarism," the population factor would be one more factor in the requirement of economic prediction. Therefore, population should constitute an element of operability within the necessary requirements to ensure economic growth, which is considered mandatory. For this school, the size and distribution of the population is a programmable factor in accordance with economic requirements.

On the other hand, we have the attempts to legitimize a "population biology" by certain authors who, like Paul Ehrlich, thought that the human character of the population is nothing more than a species distinction with respect to other animal or plant populations. For this perspective, ecology, as a subdiscipline of biology, has an interspecies approach that must be independent of anthropocentric approaches.

These "disciplinarisms" often result in biased, if not clearly erroneous, views. The most palpable example was the assumed and erroneous belief that population increase was the greatest demographic problem facing humanity. The famous Kissinger report of 1973 shows that the spread of this belief was conditioned by supremacist interests.

Population increase has not been a demographic problem; the problem has been, and is, demographic imbalance. Demographic data, by themselves, hardly enunciate value judgments, hence, it implies a certain amount of audacity to pronounce lightly on whether the increase, or on the contrary, the decrease and aging of the population, is something positive or negative in global terms. However, we can point out the problems related to technology needs, the level of consumption and the occupation of space in the environments considered, based on the comparison of statistical results. The truth is that we do not know how much is to be many and how much is to be few. Therefore, what demographic studies indicate, at most, is that in certain situations and with certain trends, certain types of problems may be encountered.

Historical experience shows us that the demographic factor that has caused the most social changes, sometimes abrupt and dramatic, has been the imbalance manifested in two dimensions: the disproportion between population and the resources-technology binomial on the one hand, and the inequality of demographic concentration in geographically close areas on the other. Hence, the relevant question is to know to what extent the demographic imbalance will affect us by studying it based on these two dimensions.

The process of urbanization, the consolidation of the national state and the improvement of bureaucracy and control mechanisms, which have taken place over the last two centuries, have made the natural movement of population on the planet practically impossible. There is no free movement of people. In many cases political borders have become barriers, retaining walls for the defense of acquired benefits. The population of the planet is spatially stagnant, and this leads to an exponential increase in imbalance.

It is logical to think that a healthy demographic policy, both locally and globally, should focus on the gradual reduction of the imbalance. To this end, in our opinion, we must tend toward a uniform distribution of the population and a stabilization of the fertility rate around the planetary average. This implies encouraging the spread of densities through free movement, which must naturally be uniform and global although gradual, and the adoption, in the case of Europe and other places with a relative fertility deficit, of pronatalist policies, until a minimum equilibrium is achieved in this respect.

The history of human population evolution has been written based on dependencies marked by historical milestones. It is to these events that we owe the abrupt jumps or steps that have led to certain population increases or regressions. In fact, many authors have strongly conditioned the population to these historical events, to the point of seeing the population increase in the so-called demographic transitions as unequivocally determined by technological and cultural progress concentrated in certain key moments.

In a society that is economically global and culturally and geopolitically interdependent, the most appropriate methodological perspective must be adopted. Thus, the macro-perspective and micro-demographic studies must always be sustained within the framework of the global analysis of general or planetary population trends. There are no absolute demographic optimums. In demography, we can only speak relatively, in the understanding that a biunivocal balance is sought in the two dimensions mentioned, and based on these two dimensions, imbalances are produced today at a world level that have repercussions of an economic and geopolitical nature.

However, it is reasonable to think that there are demographic limits and that the planet's carrying capacity is not unlimited for any given time, but it is totally unreasonable to establish arbitrary demographic optimums, if the availability of new technologies and the geopolitical configuration that prevents the free movement of people are immovable. This is why many of the demographic predictions made to date have been proven wrong.

The myth of overpopulation and population explosion, launched by Paul R. Ehrlich and propagated by Henry Kissinger, was not a scientific concept, but an ideological one. The population of the planet is growing, particularly in developing countries, while in some developed countries the last stage of the demographic transition has degenerated into a demographic implosion, which means an exponential increase in the imbalance. This imbalance, however, is not of a geo-demographic nature but is fundamentally economic and dignity-based. Increasingly, many people are asking themselves why a certain system of production and consumption is taken for granted and everything else must be adapted to its requirements, and why, on the contrary, the production and consumption system and the power structures that sustain it are not based on the human base, adapting to it. It is the world economy that must be adapted and subordinated to the people and their freedom, and not the other way around.

No one doubts that, even if the world population were to stop growing today, environmental problems would continue to threaten the survival of life as we know it, in the absence of other notable changes. Both the position that denies the incidence of population imbalance or growth, and that which points to it as the main cause of environmental deterioration, are mistaken. Both are too ideologically charged.

A vigorous leadership is needed in these matters, and particularly in what refers to migratory population movements, which implies, in many cases, a change of direction from the current one, generating collective interest to bring, and not only to "let pass" the convenient and necessary population to alleviate existing imbalances. To this end, we believe that it would be appropriate to strengthen local (municipal) decision-making in the distribution of immigrant population, with the establishment of appropriate minimum quotas, and a shift in foreign policy toward a culture of acceptance, betting on the multilateral practice of free movement in the terms and forms deemed appropriate.

Demographic policies through incentives are necessary. And there are some that are unbalancing or, on the contrary, suitable for guaranteeing the viability of the future: it is a question of choosing the right ones. Their positive consequences can be guessed: the end of the barbarism of excluding nationalism, the end of geographical determinism, and of the separation or spatial segregation of people, the advantages of transculturality, a concreteness far from multicultural syncretism by affirming the existence of values that promote cultural improvement, and a healthy balance between town and country.

All this implies, in our opinion, an arduous work of education and persuasion so that democratic pressure influences the pertinent decision-making bodies and avoids presentism. Like the family perspective, the defense of the demographic balance will result from a good imagination of the scenario to come. Chesterton said that tradition was the democracy of the dead. Here we can say that these two perspectives, that of family and that of demographic balance, are the democracy of those who will come after us.

20. Caesar and God

THE SACRALIZATION OF THE modern state by assuming quasi-religious roles, apart from attacking religious freedom, renders notable dysfunctions to the exercise of freedom. In the title, we refer to that phrase found in the Gospels of Matthew, Mark, and Luke with which Jesus Christ answers a question from the Pharisees and Herodians: "render unto Caesar the things that are Caesar's, and unto God the things that are God's" (Matt 22:21; Mark 12:17; Luke 20:25). Much has been said about this phrase in the Gospels of Matthew, Mark, and Luke.

Much has been said about this phrase, perhaps too much. I remember a book in which a whole political theory, supposedly Christian, is developed based on this phrase alone. It seems to me that this is going too far, but, in any case, the quote has a pertinent reflection, both from the profane and the sacred point of view, and sociologists who, among other areas, are dedicated to the sociology of religion, I think we have something to say about it. I personally defend that this passage in the Gospels has to be understood in conjunction with two other statements, which are the one in which Jesus says to someone who claims to be a judge in worldly matters, "Who made me a judge among you?" (Luke 12:14) and then the other in the Gospel of John when Jesus says, "My kingdom is not of this world" (John 18:36).

But let us focus on "render to Caesar what is Caesar's and to God what is God's," pointing out a confusion that I would like to clear up. It is, for people who read that phrase today, equating the concept of Caesar with the state. In my opinion they are different things. In the times in which Jesus lived the "Roman state" did not engage in what a modern state does today. It did not have a ministry of education, nor a ministry of health: the state was something else, and it was not only something else from the practical point of view, but also from the theoretical point of view. The distinction I want to emphasize is that which separates Caesarism from statism: the Caesarism of the old regime and the statism of the new regime.

Statism is exaggerated, extreme, in totalitarianism, while Caesarism is extreme in absolutism. In history, this passage from the old to the new regime, this emergence of the state as we consider it today, is due to the implementation of a bureaucratic rationality that is subject to laws that are independent of the arbitrary authority that administers and that does not only intervene in the public sphere. On the other hand, Caesarism, whose exaggeration we have already said is absolutism, is a power in act subject to arbitrariness that enables a specific person to intervene in the public. We can say that the state is the political dress of a collectivity, while Caesarism is the political dress with which an absolute power, more or less great, endows itself. But the ideal types are different, Caesarism on the one hand and statism on the other.

I have sometimes wondered if I, as a victim, had the opportunity to choose between one of these two exaggerations, which one I would choose. Well, I would choose absolutism, because it would give me more freedom. Totalitarianism gets inside you and forces you to think in a certain way. Absolutism goes as far as it goes, but it cannot go any further. That expression attributed to *The Sun King* that "the state is me" does not mean that Louis XIV understood the state as we understand it now. What he said, if he said it at all, is that when he is there, what is the need for a state, and when Caesar is there, what is the need for a state, as if to support the idea that there are two ways. These two paths are clearly separated in the passage from the old to the new regime. In the old regime the relationship between the temporal power of Caesar and the spiritual power of the churches was seen differently than in the new regime.

Referring to the power of the state and the power of the churches, different stages have been passed through with different steps. In the old regime the theory of St. Augustine prevailed, the interpretation of the two cities and of harmony in primacy. All authority comes from God and there is a separation between temporal power and spiritual power, the latter assuming a theoretical but not practical primacy. In the end, when the modern era came and the state, the Caesar at that time, was obliged to manifest a confessionalism in its territory, we arrive at this obtuse formula of "the religion of the king is the religion of the people," which was brought by Protestantism.

In the new regime, which follows, confessionalism is understood in a different way, as something more lax. The state can be confessional, but the state does not necessarily impose the same religion on all subjects. In the process of the relations of independence or coexistence between church and state in the new regime, confessionally is followed, later on, by a juridical separation with great dissimilarities between countries. This separation was culminated by the Catholic Church (other churches did not), and the Second Vatican Council stipulated a church-state separation which, among other things, banished confessionalism and prohibited the clergy from participating in the government of temporal affairs. Logically, a second separation was also to be expected, and this is where I would like to make a point right now, a separation of the state from the sacred, but this separation is still pending, because one of the characteristics of the relationship between temporal power and spiritual power today, at the end of modernity, is the sacralization of the state.

The modern state advocates a civil religion. It endows itself with a quasi-religious authority. There is a cult, there is a liturgy, and there are secular rites: a whole symbolism and a ceremonial, as if the state were proposed as another church. There are officiants, there is iconization of symbols, of the flag of the nation, even something that also reaches sports, with hymns, chants, flags, and that in the opening and closing ceremonies of the Olympic Games, it seems as if this sacralization of the public gave the message that the state is the owner of that sphere, of the public. This is not true; it is a dysfunctional political aspiration.

We need religion and, therefore, this pending separation of the state from the sacred must be brought to the present as soon as possible. The question asked by the Pharisees and Herodians to Jesus, "Should we or should we not pay tribute to Caesar?" and the answer of Jesus, "Give to Caesar what is Caesar's and to God what is God's," should perhaps be posed differently today. In my view, seeing whether we must give back to God what is God's. The sociology of religion has studied these matters, more or less correctly, and one believes that indeed the state has to give back to God what is God's, that is to say: the sacred. And to give it back it must find the subject to which it is given back, and that subject is the churches. Instead of usurping their place, states should make room for the churches to operate in the public sphere as well.

In the treatment of this issue in the sociology of religion there are divergent schools. I stand with authors such as Rodney Stark or José Casanova, and there is a contrast between what they advocate and what another school of sociologists, among whom we can name Émile Durkheim and Peter Berger, advocate. In my opinion both were wrong in some of their approaches in this respect. Durkheim talked a lot about religion, but mentioned God very little, something that Stark tries to correct with a book entitled *Why God*, where he calls for the divine to be contemplated in sociological discourse. Durkheim was also wrong when he said that the gods appeared in society much later than religion did. This distinction between the divine and the religious, which we find in the French pioneer, is a distinction which, in my opinion and in the opinion of Stark and other sociologists, is not appropriate. On the other hand, Peter Berger erred in contrasting pluralism with religious vigor, and in saying that secularization was the same as desacralization. This is not true because, among other things, Berger ignored the de-supernaturalization from within the churches, and how this influenced what today is understood as a process of secularization, which, in my opinion, must be placed in parallel with the processes of religification as we have discussed, together with professors Javier Ros, Tomás Baviera, and Javier Aznar, in *Sociology of Religious Experience*.

Regarding Caesar and God, it is worth speaking of religious freedom. Without religious freedom there is no freedom that is worthwhile, and, in my opinion, this freedom is the most important thermometer that we have to evaluate the political quality of a society. If the state can enter the most intimate sphere of people, which is belief, the state has already gone too far. That is why the question of what we should give back to God is an urgent and crucial one. The desacralization of the state and its withdrawal from all its pomp, ceremony, and quasi-religious rites is necessary for the well-being of civil society, for political well-being, and for the peace and security of any society.

There is no doubt that, at the same time, the necessary de-statization of the church(es) is necessary for religion to increase its social functionality. In the case of countries with Catholic roots, this requires the defense of a genuine Christian secularity in tune with the requirements of the faith and its mission. The desacralization of the state and the de-statization of the church are parallel social optimums.

In addition, a prior and necessary distinction must be made here. From the point of view of our discipline, it would be appropriate to emphasize the importance of the plural subject in religious discourse. This is something pertinent and we will try to defend the plural subject, even if it seems, at first sight, that it leads us to justify an even greater nationalization of the church. As we will see later, this is not so, but let us begin by seeing how the plural subject in religious discourse has been poorly understood. Jesus usually speaks to us in the plural, specifically when he says, "Give or give all of you. . . ." He also does so on many other occasions such as when he teaches us to pray and says "our Father" instead of "my Father," or when the church proposes "pray for us" instead of "pray for me." Jesus, in the Gospel, often addresses the collective and he judges collectivities. He understands the collectivity as a moral subject, as we can see in the anti-beatitudes that follow the beatitudes, or in the curses in the gospel. It casts curses on collective entities such as cities like Chorazin, Bethsaida, or Capernaum. And in the primitive church it is done in the same way and letters are addressed to cities.

Apart from the letters that the Apostle Paul may address to the Corinthians, to those of Thessalonica, etc., in the apocalypse, the author of the text begins by addressing seven cities: the churches of Ephesus, Smyrna, Pergamum, Thyatira, Tardis, Philadelphia, and Laodicea. But not content with this testimony of the recognition of plural subjects as moral subjects, the church has recently spoken to us about something that has even appeared scandalous to some, namely the defense of social sin, already mentioned by Pope John Paul II in a document called "Reconciliation and Penance," in 1989. Before, we had original sin, but now we hear more specifically about social sin and, not content with that, the same pope, as we have already recalled, in 1987 in the encyclical *Sollicitudo rei socialis* also spoke to us about the structures of sin. Some liberals tore their garments trying to correct the pontiff by saying that sin can only be personal and individual. Well, no: there are also structures of sin and there is also social sin.

To me, this seems easy to understand, if one understands that we can also sin by omission, and that there is complicity in certain collective sins. Now, collectivities in the globalized and interconnected world are more affirmed than ever, and if one thinks of those collective punishments for personal sins narrated in the Bible, one is surprised by the liberal scandal. Collective sin is not the sum of personal sins, because collectivity is not the sum of individualities. As has always been explained, the collectivity is what is left when you take away the individualities. Well, all this seems as if it would lead to a necessary foundation of the church as an organization that takes care of collectivities, the believers, and that it should take care of them for salvation. Well, this is something that we want to refute here, because what we want to talk about is precisely the opposite: the necessary de-statization of the church.

How can we sociologists speak, one might ask, of the necessary de-statization of the church, if at the same time we defend social sins or collectivities as moral subjects? The distinction to be made now is between the clerical and the lay within the church. The public expression of the religious points us to collective responsibilities, but responsibilities that can be understood from the point of view of what we are going to defend here, which is a Christian secularity.

To understand what Christian secularity can be, we must adopt an eminently secular vision or paradigm, in a positive sense, not a clerical one. The faithful in the church are supposed to be either clerics or laity; well, a paradigm or a lay way of understanding would underpin that pillar that we call Christian secularity that we present as an alternative to the statization of the church. One thinks that all this would be easy to understand, if in addition to having read the gospel with the eyes of a philosopher, theologian, or as many have done, a social worker, one had also read it with the eyes of a sociologist, something that here and now we are vindicating.

At the beginning of Christianity, we believe it was like that, those words of Jesus referring to collectives, the letters of the apostles, or in the apocalypse, which referred to cities as subjects of virtue and as subjects of vices or sins, were fresh. And in early Christianity there are some authors who are tremendously interesting, and that I think it is pertinent to highlight, because they also bring up this issue, that there is a morality, and there is a vice, and there is a sin that are of a collective nature. We speak, fundamentally, of Eusebius of Caesarea and Saint Justin. The latter is one of my favorite saints, and he was a layman, teacher, and martyr. He is the author of the *Dialogue with Trypho*, and some also point to him as the author of the *Epistle to Diognetus*, although this is quite debated. Eusebius of Caesarea is the author of the *Ecclesiastical History*, from which I will not spare myself from quoting a paragraph in which he blames the church itself, the collectivity of all Christians, for the strongest persecution that was unleashed in the first centuries with Diocletian. It reads as follows:

> As we began to abandon ourselves to negligence and carelessness due to the misuse of so many years of freedom, and some to envy and criticize others; as we made war on each other, wounding each other by word as weapons and spears; as prelates fought against prelates and peoples against peoples raising revolts and tumults; finally, as fraud and deceit prevailed to the point of malice, then the divine justice began to admonish us first with gentle embrace as usual almost without feeling and moderately without yet touching the general body of the church and the multitudes of the faithful still being able to gather freely; then the persecution broke out in its beginnings by those who exercised the militia.[1]

Everyone's fault and divine punishment, a persecution that Eusebius himself suffered, although he did not die in it. What an interesting and, in my opinion, healthy perspective. We are all church. In the church, there are clergy and laity on an equal footing. We are all equal children of God to whom we answer not only individually, but also collectively.

If before we had asked ourselves what we have to give back to God and specifically what the state has to give back to God in this process of desacralization, now it is pertinent to ask ourselves what we have to give back to Caesar in the process of de-statization of the church. And I say well to Caesar and not to the state, because what had to be returned to the state has

1. Velasco-Delgado, *Eusebio de Cesarea*, 521.

already been returned in that separation of church and state, the temporal and the spiritual, sanctioned in the Vatican Council. The separation of the state from the sacred, however, as we have pointed out, is still pending. But how can we give back to Caesar what is Caesar's, give back to society what is society's, from the ecclesial point of view? Through Christian secularity. We must give back prominence both in the church and outside it to the figure of the secular, of the layperson.

The Christian layperson has a responsibility that the church must respect in his or her work in the public sphere, representing the church through this work, something that is not only the responsibility of the clergy. In the so-called profane spheres, it is the laity who should bear witness to the church, and this is the process of de-stabilization of the church: transferring lay power. To understand the hierarchy in another way, not as an endless series of steps and orders, but simply as two estates: the vicar of Christ and his representatives, the bishops, and the faithful people, clergy and laity in equality. Distinction of functions but without distinction of category as children of God.

The process of de-statization of the church, which should go hand in hand with the desacralization of the state, is a process to be completed, especially in practice. It is a necessity if religious freedom is to be recognized as the foundation of all other freedoms. We already stated this some time ago in *The Fourth Christianity*, a proposal with concrete policies for the de-statization of the church, which we believe is still relevant today. Christian secularity and a positive Christian secularism are the answer to the question we have asked ourselves as to how we can give back to Caesar, from the point of view of religion and religious institutions, what is due. And, dare I say, here too is pointed out the need for serious sociological preparation among those who are engaged in studying theology and preparing to enter the ranks of the clerical function.

Epilogue

WE BEGAN THIS BOOK talking about theoretical morality and concluded it on practical morality. As I have been completing the various chapters, my reading appetite has not ceased. As one reads many of the new ideas coming through, ponder on the ones already settled, bringing to the fore in the question of whether it would be worthwhile to change this or that. If one were to make way for all these questions one would never finish a book. That is to say that all texts are unconcluded and that the writer as a matter of expedience leaves the conclusion for a forthcoming work.

That is not my case here for I do not wish to write another scholarly book. I must say that I am satisfied with what I have written even if I know that if I were to write this book again, I would say some things differently. In any case and as we remember, someone said: "What is written is written."

That notwithstanding, I think I should call the attention at the end of the book to some things that I consider bear more weight in the discourse we are concluding. When talking about the society to come, about what is missing and what must be left over to reach a sustainable and dignified collective way of life, it is necessary to stop and think about the who: us now. Will we be able to do it? No one doubts it, and I, even though I find it difficult, have no choice but to say that it is possible, that we will be able to do it . . . if we realize it. The conditioning factor is, however, immense.

And not just because of how much we ought to unthink, collectively speaking, reversing the inertia of modern errors, but because, sadly, the state of intellectual prostration and demoralization of the subject, us, that must realize, is lamentable. Never have we been so bad (self-deceived, dominated, and dispossessed) and never before has it been more urgent for us to be well (failure can end time).

Well, all right, but some could say that this is the cold analysis of an intellectual who discourses rationally within the channels of propositional reasonableness. In Palladian Latin: with good words we are not going

anywhere. That we are not going to pass by magic from playful self-deception to the radical reform of styles, forms, and purposes of life is, in my
opinion, clear. That we do not have time to enlighten the dispossessed about
the goodness of self-possession before unfeasibility knocks at the door, I
think, in my opinion, too, is so. But I also think that, regardless of the state
of anomie, alienation, hallucination, or despondency of the who, the who
can be awakened from their lethargy by actions or events totally unforeseen
and unforeseeable from and with the kind of analysis and prospective academic elucidation we are accustomed to.

Modernity appeared through a change of regime, which in some
places took the form of revolution rather than reform. And I don't think we
should close the door to that possibility now. No, I am not talking about a
bloody revolution, but about an inner revolution, which I believe is capable
of impersonating those who, moved by a transcendent purpose and in the
face of an unforeseen and lacerating event, make the conscious decision to
break with modernity and its structures of power and domination.

What is at stake is precisely reality. We must strip it of its adornments,
disguises, trappings, pomp, cover-ups, artifice, and virtuality in order to
find ourselves in it as we are. To be able to look in its mirrors and discover
who we are, unique and different, and, as such, to recognize others for what
they are worth. Enriched and enriching in an environment that was there
without us realizing it.

In my opinion, this means dismantling, under the protection of the
law, the communication and information monopolies that, through the
control of invisible algorithms, co-opt wills and subvert established democracies. And it also happens because civil society believes itself to be
the protagonist of its own destiny, beyond the protection, the umbrella of
the state. It is a two-sided bet in which the state must win and conquer,
and then, metaphorically, be defeated and surrender itself. To overcome the
market without empowerment itself surrendering to the civil to save and
underpin a responsible civility. The state must confront the market and the
community must grow so that, in the end, there can be that balance between
market, state, and community that would be desirable.

I don't think we have much time to lose. And we can always start with
ourselves.

Acknowledgments

AT THIS POINT IN life, one of the feelings that first arises in the accounting of debts is gratitude, which sometimes goes hand in hand with regret for not having made it explicit at the time. I should thank so many people who have made it possible that, despite my many miseries and failures, I have been able to write and, in the end, after many others, to publish this book. I have not explicitly thanked them before, so you will forgive me for doing so now. I make no distinction between those who suffer in this world and those who enjoy eternity (already quite a few), since they fit equally in my memory. I have decided not to exceed six lines per paragraph, so I regret, with pain, not being able to include so many others who, I hope for your approval and understanding, can forgive their absence in print.

From my academic life I must mention Duncan Waterson, my thesis director, for his exquisite and kind liberality; Amitai Etzioni, for his leadership and recognition; Mariano Artigas, Federico Suárez, Vicente Cacho, Cormac Burke, and Jutta Burggraf for their teaching and solicitous care; Fernando Fernández for his dedication and selflessness; Antoni Jutglar for his courage and foresight; and Manning Clark for his originality.

Among those who have helped me in various endeavors that have opened my mind to the needs of others, I must name Jesús Poveda, Rosario Athié, Ana Tere López de Llergo, Hugo Obiglio, Richard and Rosemarie Stith, Dolores Voltas, Justo Aznar, José Eugenio Arnau, Ana Otte, Concha Medialdea, Vicente Oltra, Jesús and Amparo Ballesteros, Vicente Bellver, Pedro Talavera, Jorge Scala, Paco León, and Rafael Cabrera.

From my domestic life, I must mention those who did more than their share of taking care of me in a special way. There are, apart from my grandmother Elisa, all those women who, with their quiet dedication and devotion in the service of the houses where I have lived, have made it possible for me to work at ease. There is not room for all of them, so I will name two that I remember with great affection: Carmen Lobán and Consuelo Sanz.

And finally, those I have known only through their work. To the authors of *El Persiles*, *The Ball and the Cross*, *El libro de Sigüenza*, *Viaje a pie*, *Por tierras de Portugal y España*, *El Criticón*, *Memorias inmemoriales*, *Libro de la vida*, *The Confessions*, *Extremeñas*, *Utopia*, *Las flores del bien*, *La Cristiada*, *Anarchy and Order*, *Being and Having*, *Man and the State*, *El Criterio*, and *Le réalisme méthodique*.

To all of them, for great undeserved favors, thank you very much. From so much, so little.

References

(year of the Spanish edition, when available)

Anders, Gunther, *La obsolescencia del hombre I y II*, 2011.

Aristotle, *Nicomachean Ethics*, 2014.

Augustine of Hippo, *The City of God*, 2019.

Baier, Annette, *Moral Prejudices: Essays on Ethics*, 1995.

Baum, Gregory, *Religion and Alienation: Theological Reading of Sociology*, 1980.

Beck, Ulrich, *La Sociedad del Riesgo*, 1990.

Benedict XVI, "Address at the University of Regensburg," September 12, 2006.

———, "Address in Westminster Hall," September 17, 2010.

———, "Homily in Regensburg," September 12, 2006.

———, "Speech in the German Parliament," September 22, 2011.

Berry, Wendell, *What Are People For*, 1990.

Boudon, Roger, *"Le juste et le vrai": Ètudes sur lóbjectivité des valeurs et de la connaissance*, 1995.

Buchanan, James, *Constitutional Economics*, 1993.

Burgos, Juan Manuel, *Repensar la Naturaleza Humana*, 2006.

Calderón de la Barca, Pedro, *La Vida es Sueño*, 1635.

Casanova, José, *Public Religions in the Modern World*, 1994.

Chaunu, Pierre, *History and Decline*, 1983.

Crouch, Colin, *Post-Democracy*, 2000.

Dostoevsky, Fyodor, *The Brothers Karamazov*, 1880.

Durkheim, Émile, *The Elementary Forms of Religious Life*, 1912.

Elias, Norbert, *The Civilizing Process*, 1939.

Etzioni, Amitai, *The Moral Dimension*, 1988.

———, *My Brother's Keeper*, 2003.

Fayol, Henri, *Industrial and General Management*, 1916.

Frankfurt, Harry, *On Inequality*, 2015.

Fukuyama, Francis, *The End of History and the Last Man*, 1992.

Gomá, Javier, *Tetralogía de la Ejemplaridad*, 2010.

Han, Byung-Chul, *La expulsión de lo distinto*, 2017.

Havel, Vaclav, *The Power of the Powerless*, 2013.

Hegel, G. W. F., *Writings on Religion*, 2013.

Illouz, Eva, *Consuming the Romantic Utopia*, 1997.

Jenkins, Philip, *The New Anti-Catholicism*, 2005.

———, *The Next Christendom: The Coming of Global Christianity*, 2002.

John Paul II, *Sollicitudo Rei Socialis*, 1987.

Jonas, Hans, *The Imperative of Responsibility*, 1979.

Kant, Immanuel, *The Metaphysics of Morals*, 2012.

Lope de Vega, *Fuenteovejuna*, 1613.

MacDonald, Dwight, *The Root Is Man*, 1946.

MacIntyre, Alasdair, *Dependent Rational Animals*, 2001.

Marías, Julián, *Tratado de lo mejor*, 1995.

McLuhan, Marshall, *The Global Village*, 1964.

Melich, Joan-Carles, *Filosofía de la finitud*, 2002.

Morin, Edgar, *L'home et la mort*, 1951.

Mumford, Lewis, *The Culture of Cities*, 1945.

Nisbet, Robert, *History of the Idea of Progress*, 1980.

Ostrom, Elinor, *Governing the Commons*, 2011.

Pareto, Vilfredo, *Sociological Writings*, 1987.

Pérez-Adán, José, "La cuarta cristiandad," in *Anales Valentinos Revista de Filosofía y Teología*, 2012.

———. *Pasar el testigo*, 2020.

———, *Pequeña investigación sobre la caridad política*, 2017.

———, *La Salud Social*, 1999.

———, *Sobrepoder*, 2016.

Pérez-Adán, José, Javier Aznar, and Javier Ros, *Sociología de la Experiencia Religiosa*, 2018.

Rorty, Richard, *An Ethics for Today*, 2009.

Rosa, Hartmut, *Resonance: A Sociology of Our Relationship to the World*, 2019.

Rosanvallon, Pierre, *La sociedad de los iguales*, 2012.

Samuelson, Paul, *The Foundations of Modern Economics*, 1974.

Schumacher, E. F., *Small Is Beautiful*, 1973.

Sen, Amartya, *Development as Freedom*, 1999.

Sennett, Richard, *The Craftsman*, 2008.

Smith, Adam, *Theory of Moral Sentiments*, 1979.

Stark, Rodney, *The Victory of Reason*, 2005.

Taylor, F. W., *Principles of Scientific Management Theory*, 1911.

Tönnies, Ferdinand, *Community and Society*, 1887.

Toynbee, Arnold, *A Study of History*, 1933–1961.

Velasco-Delgado, Argimiro, *Eusebio de Cesarea: Historia Eclesiástica*, 2008.

Vernadsky, Vladimir, *La biosfera*, 1926.

Weber, Max, *Economy and Society*, 1922.

———, *The Protestant Ethic and the Spirit of Capitalism*, 1905.

www.ingramcontent.com/pod-product-compliance
Lightning Source LLC
Chambersburg PA
CBHW030844270326
41928CB00007B/1201